GLOBAL WARRIOR

THE STORY OF

GROUP CAPTAIN J.R.JEUDWINE

DSO OBE DFC

by

ALAIN CHARPENTIER

LIONEL LACEY-JOHNSON
and
GEOFFREY JEUDWINE

Published in 1999 by
L. Lacey-Johnson

Printed ,Bound and Cover Design © in England by

Kall Kwik
68 Terminus Road
Eastbourne
BN21 3LX

ISBN 0- 9536418- 0- 5

GLOBAL WARRIOR

Contents

Acknowledgements

Editorial and Glossary

Bibliography.

ACKNOWLEDGEMENTS

The research and gathering of information for this book has provided the authors with the opportunity, not only to expand their knowledge of Royal Air Force history, but to meet and enjoy the company of many very kind and helpful people. We wish to express our sincere thanks to those organisations which have been approached for help, namely the Air Historical Branch of the Ministry of Defence in London, the archives section of the Royal Air Force Museum, the Public Records Office, The Royal Air Force College Cranwell, the RAF Personnel Management Centre and numerous Squadron Associations. We are particularly grateful for the help, loan of photographs and provision of anecdotes from the following individuals who were able to contribute in one way or another to this remarkable story :-
Nonie Beckingsale, Tim Hills, Elisabeth Hutton-Squire, Bob Tozer, the secretary of the Old Shirburnian Society, for the provision of some family history. Captain Sutton CBE DSC, Ray Sturtivant and John Winton for the background to HMS "Glorious". Wg Cdr Arthur Gill DFC OBE, Peter Haynes OBE, David Russell, the late Flt Lt John Wylie DFC, Michelle Lovkiss, daughter of Athel Snook, who helped with the Far East saga, also to Don Neate, author of "Scorpion's Sting" and Christopher Shores and Brian Cull authors of "Bloody Shambles", for permission to quote from their works. Sqn Ldr Norman Orr, Ron Fuller, Bob Watkins and Sqn Ldr Tony Plinston DFC for their part in chapter 3. Flt Lt Jack Howard DFC, Alec Bates, Leslie Birch DFM and Flt Lt John Whitely, secretary of the 619 Sqn Association, Wg Cdr R.A. Milward OBE DFC, Robert Owen, Steve Vessey and many others who helped with the chapter on Bomber Command; and last but not least Mr Alan Simpson, Dennis Pell and Sgt Peter Stanley RAF who all assisted with the tragic end of the story.

Alain Charpentier
Lionel Lacey-Johnson
Geoffrey Jeudwine

EDITORIAL

Although not without precedent, having three people writing one story does perhaps require a few words of explanation. The idea of the book originated with Alain Charpentier. As the youngest member of our team, Alain is a very keen aviation historian, who has devoted much of his life to researching the circumstances in which many Allied aircraft crashed in France during the Second World War. In the course of his painstaking efforts he has contacted many survivors and relatives of the airmen who died in these crashes, and his actions have led to many reunions and, with the aid of local dignitaries, to the holding of several memorial services throughout central France. Alain has also written several detailed accounts of raids by Allied aircraft on German targets in France. One such raid was on a German ammunition dump at Salbris, and it was during the course of writing this account that he realised that Wing Commander Jeudwine had been an exceptional pilot and commander. It became clear that every effort should be made to find out more about this extraordinary airman.

Geoffrey Jeudwine, John's younger cousin, lives in Queensland Australia. In the course of researching his family history he made contact with Monsieur Charpentier and, later, with myself. Living closer to the scene of what might be described as "the Far East saga", it occurred to Alain and myself that Geoffrey was better placed to write that part of the story and we invited him to do just that. With much hard work and some luck he has been able to obtain first hand accounts from survivors of the remarkable escape from Java in the ship's lifeboat, which they named the "Scorpion".

For my part I have concentrated on Jeudwine's early days at school and in the Royal Air Force and, because I have some first hand knowledge of the Egyptian desert, I have written about John's involvement in the now famous battle of Alamein.

I have had the added responsibility of editing the work of all three authors. I have tried to mould our different styles into some sort of readable material, to standardise forms of abbreviations and nomenclature and to decide on forms of layout and print size. With the best will in the world I know that I will not have been entirely successful in all this and I apologise in advance for my mistakes. Some mistakes in abbreviations, particularly of ranks, in the spelling of names, and the recording of time and dates, may be excused by the fact that many of these things have changed over the years, and many of the official records were written by clerical staff who were under immense pressure at the time.

Finally, the variation in Christian names and titles needs some explanation. Jeudwine was christened John Raymond Jeudwine, his family generally referred to him as Raymond but in the Royal Air Force he was known as John. His niece, Nonie Beckingsale, referred to him as uncle "Judy" and that nickname was used by a few of his subordinates, while others called him "The Skipper" or "The Winco". Wherever ranks are used they mostly refer to the rank held at the time of a particular event.

L.L-J

GLOSSARY

AA	Anti Aircraft
AM	Air ministry
AM/WT	Air Ministry/Wireless Transmission
AOC	Air Officer Commanding
Chop Night	A night in which many aircraft were lost
Code Letter	Letters given to aircraft for identification
Cookie	4,000lb bomb
Crossbow	Raid against German V Weapon targets
D Day	6th June 1944. Allied landings in Normandy
DF	Direction finding (Radio)
Enigma	German coding machine
Flak	Fliegerabwehrkannonen-German anti aircraft fire
Gardening	Mine laying sorties
H2S	British airborne radar navigation aid
HCU	Heavy Conversion Unit -usually two to four engines
LG	Landing Ground
Newhaven	Target marking using H2S
Nickel	Leaflet dropping operations
NJG	Nachjagdeschwader. German night fighter wing
Oboe	Blind bombing/Navigation aid
OTU	Operational Training Unit
Overlord	Codeword for Allied Invasion of Europe
Panzer	German tank
PFF	Pathfinder Force
PI	Photo Interpretation (Interpreter)
PR	Photo reconnaissance
RAAF	Royal Australian Air Force
RT	Radio transmission (Voice)
SABS	Stabilised Automatic Bomb Sight
SAAF	South African Air Force

Squadron 540.	RAF Squadron Operational Record Book
Sigint	Intelligence derived from enemy radio signals
Tallboy	12,000lb bomb
TSR	Torpedo Spotter and Reconnaissance
SOE	Special Operations Executive
Ultra	Decoded Enigma messages
USAAF	United States Army Air Force
USAMEAF	United States Army Middle East Air Force
WAAF	Woman's Auxiliary Air Force
Window	Strips of aluminium foil dropped to jam enemy radar
WOP/AG	Wireless Operator/Air Gunner
WT	Wireless transmission (Morse)
V1/V2	German rocket weapons
Y Service	Monitoring of enemy radio communications

Abbreviations of RAF Officer Ranks used in this book-

AM	Air Marshal
AVM	Air Vice Marshal
A/Cdre	Air Commodore
Gp Capt	Group Captain
Wg Cdr	Wing Commander
Sqn Ldr	Squadron Leader
Flt Lt	Flight Lieutenant
Fg Offr	Flying Officer
Plt Offr	Pilot Officer

FOREWORD

by Wing Commander A.M. Gill OBE DFC AE RAF

I am honoured to have been invited to write the foreword to this book about a professional aviator and one of my former commanding officers whom I greatly admired and respected. When I first met Wing Commander John Raymond Jeudwine on the 5th January 1942, he had just arrived at Heliopolis airfield near Cairo Egypt, as the newly appointed Squadron Commander of No 84 Bomber Squadron of the Royal Air Force. I was not over-impressed, he was tall, slim, well cut but very quiet. The squadron had just been withdrawn from the Western Desert after a successful campaign, to re-equip with new or reconditioned Bristol Blenheim MkIV light bombers, prior to being transferred to the Far East to fight the Japanese. I was then a young Flying Officer (acting Flight Lieutenant) who had just completed 26 operational sorties against General Rommel's Africa Corps and the Italians.

But how very wrong were my first impressions!. John Jeudwine's quiet approach to the problems which faced him, of which there were many, was in marked contrast to that of his predecessor, who was a robust "driver of men". John had been a signals specialist in the Middle East with no operational flying experience and with only a few flying hours on the Blenheim. But I quickly discovered that, behind that quiet, unassuming exterior, there was a man of great determination, drive and a born leader.

As you will read, No 84 Squadron had been increased in size before leaving for the Far East, from two to three flights, with a total of 33 complete aircrews, 484 ground staff and 24 aircraft. The first flight, led by Flt Lt John Wyllie and of which I had been appointed deputy flight commander, left Heliopolis on the 14th January 1942 to fly to the Far East in 10 days. John Jeudwine, as the new CO, did not leave Egypt until the 16th but, by pressing on and making up time, he caught up with the second flight at Karachi in India and the first flight at Calcutta. From there we flew together to Palembang in Sumatra where we landed on the 23rd. What happened after that makes interesting reading.

All those who read this book will owe a debt of gratitude to Lt Col Lionel Lacey-Johnson in England, Alain Charpentier in France and Geoffrey Jeudwine (John's younger cousin) in Australia for their dedicated research over a long period of time into the life of a man who might otherwise have been ignored and forgotten-except by those who were priviledged to have served under him during the Second World War.

I always felt that John Jeudwine was a very private, almost a lonely man, who did not mix easily and who sometimes appeared ill at ease in some company. It was not until after his untimely death that I discovered his christian names. In his letters to me later in the war he always signed himself "J.R. Jeudwine" or "JRJ". But, to be fair, in those days first names were seldom used, either at school or in the services and never to one's commanding officer.

As each day passed in those hectic days in 1942, I discovered that JRJ possessed exceptional leadership qualities; far greater than those more senior than he was. He always led from the front and constantly inspired those under him by his example. He was a most considerate man and I have met very few COs with such qualities.

In Sumatra in 1942, my crew and I were part of what he called his "night flying team".On one particular night operation against the Japanese invasion forces who were landing some 60 miles North of Singapore, I had been allotted a battered old Blenheim Mk 1. After the attack we landed at Sembawang on Singapore Island to refuel. On landing I crashed when the aircraft overshot the runway in the dark due to unserviceable brakes. After his aircraft had been refuelled, John flew me and my crew back to Sumatra, squeezed into the "well" of his Blenheim; thereby probably preventing us from becoming Japanese prisoners of war, for which I will always be grateful.

I have always been a fatalist-believing that what is to be will be. That crash at night on a badly lit airfield, was the first of my 17 forced-landings and crashes during my 41 years of flying. I therefore find it extremely sad that John should have been killed as he was after such an eventful flying career and at such a young age. I believe that had he not been killed prematurely in an aircraft of which he had very little experience, he would have become an Air Marshal in the peacetime Royal Air Force. His sudden death was a great tragedy and a shock to his family and friends, and certainly a great loss to the Royal Air Force.

It is appropriate that this book should now be published because it was John's intention to write about his adventures, an ambition that sadly was never achieved. Those members of 84,55 and 619 Squadrons still living some 55 years after those fateful days will be grateful to the authors that a great warrior has been remembered with such pride and affection.

AMG

John Raymond Jeudwine
1913 - 1945

CHAPTER 1

Early Days

John Raymond Jeudwine was born at Number 7 Brooklands, Filey in Yorkshire on the 9th July 1913. His father, Wilfred Wynne Jeudwine, was described on the birth certificate as a doctor in the Indian Medical Service, but this brief description belittles a conspicuous medical career with the Indian Medical Service, during which he served on the North West Frontier, in Europe during the Great War and as a professor of ophthalmic surgery in Lahore. He was made a Companion of The Order of St Michael and St George (CMG) in 1916. Wilfred's father, George Wynne, was the one time Dean of Lincoln Cathedral, and several other members of the family led distinguished careers, including General Sir Hugh Sandham Jeudwine KCB CB, who played a prominent part in the South African Wars of 1898- 1900.

Raymond's mother,Mabel Gertrude Jeudwine, was, before her marriage, Mabel Barker, a very tall and good looking woman who was born in 1874, probably in Australia, because her father, who worked for Cable and Wireless, had moved his whole family there. Mabel was sent home to school in England and while she was away her parents died in a cholera epidemic, and she was brought up by foster parents near Frome in Dorset. She married Wilfred in India (possibly Simla) around 1903/4, and came home to England to have her three children. After Wilfred's death in 1943 she went to live first with her daughter Erica near Peterborough then to London and Worthing and finally to a Nursing Home near Salisbury, where she died in 1964. Raymond's sister Erica, who was born in June 1909 became Mrs Erica Hills and died near Swindon in January 1992. A second daughter, Joan, died as a child before Raymond was born. Erica's children (Raymond's nephew

1

and niece) have been interviewed and have helped with this story. At the age of eight Raymond, as he was known to his family, attended prep school at Crowthorne Towers, a school which fed pupils to Wellington College and Sherborne School in Dorset, the latter becoming his main school from 1927 to 1931.There are few records of his achievements at either his prep school or Sherborne, but we do know that while at Crowthorne Towers he became head of the VIth Form and was awarded a book prize in July 1926.At Sherborne, although very keen on all forms of sport, his tall and thin physique precluded his selection for the school rugby fifteen, but he did play for his House Team and was often well placed in the cross country running. He became a corporal in the school OTC and was in the school shooting team.

Between 1931 and 1932 he obviously set his sights on joining the Royal Air Force, and, after some private tuition, he gained entrance to the Royal Air Force College Cranwell via the Civil Service Commission Examination Scheme, which awarded Prize Cadetships to the three armed service colleges. The actual prize amounted to a substantial reduction in the payment of annual fees from £100 to £20, with uniform and books provided free.

Flight Cadet Jeudwine started his training at the RAF College on the 1st September 1932, joining nine other cadets in the newly formed 'C' Squadron. Sixteen months later he was promoted to Flight Cadet Sergeant , and was regularly representing the College at athletics, cross country running and fencing. He also became the sub editor of the College Journal.

The young aviator probably started his flying in the Avro Tutor, progressing to the Armstrong Whitworth Siskin, Bristol Bulldog and the Hawker Fury, all of which were in use at Cranwell at that time.The RAF in the 1930's was operating some 28 different types of aircraft from the Moth communications aircraft to the heavy Heyford bomber.

Apart from his flying training Raymond would have attended lectures on academic subjects such as General Science,

2

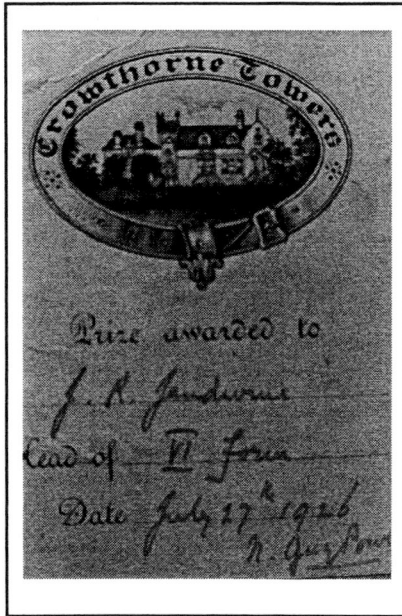

Record of prize at Crowthorne Towers

House Rugby Team 1928

Photos: Old Shirburnian Society

Aeronautical Engineering, Electricity and Wireless, Armaments and Humanitarian Subjects connected with flying. It was probable that he chose Electricity and Wireless as his special subject, as he later held several appointments in Signals Intelligence. His flying instruction included Pilot Navigation on cross country flights to such airfields as Duxford, Bircham Newton and Catterick. Instrument flying was still in a somewhat rudimentary stage, and most flights were by "seat of pants" relying on maps and close observation of ground features.

The Journal of the RAF College Cranwell for the Autumn of 1934 has several references to Raymond's achievements, in particular in the field of sports. In the annual triangular contest between the colleges of Cranwell, Sandhurst and Woolwich, Raymond is described as having had "a thrilling struggle" in the Mile event between himself and a Sandhurst cadet called Constantine, in which Raymond finished just two yards ahead of his rival in the time of 4 minutes and 35 seconds. Earlier in the year he was in the winning team in a fencing match against The Royal Military Academy, having performed well in the Bayonets class.

During his two years at Cranwell there was an official opening ceremony carried out by the Prince of Wales, who held the rank of Air Marshal. The ceremony led to the writing of the History of Cranwell -published by Gale and Polden at 2 shillings. The book contained a short history of the village of Cranwell in Saxon and Norman times, the history of the Cranwell family and recorded events at the college since its inception in the 1920s, when, as a Royal Naval Air Station, it was known as HMS Daedalus.

Flight Cadet Sergeant Jeudwine was amongst the 28 cadets who formed the Passing Out Term in the summer of 1934. All but three of his original C Squadron contemporaries appear on the photograph, and records show that Raymond had built up an above average number of credits to his name. The passing out or "Wings" parade took place on the 27th July 1934 and he was listed

"C" Squadron Cranwell 1932

Avro Tutor at Cranwell

Photos: RAF College Cranwell

5

as being 5th out of 28 in the order of merit. In his passing out report the Commandant, Air Vice Marshal W.G.S. Mitchell, described Raymond thus -"Has improved in every way and has gained self confidence to advantage. He took a keen interest in everything, and will be a valuable and capable officer of quiet character". Pilot Officer John Jeudwine, as he was to become known in the service, was posted to No 12 Bomber Squadron at the RAF Station Andover.

The Squadron Commander, Sqn Ldr A.C. Bayley , allotted his new pilot to "A" Flight where John joined four other Pilot Officers[1] flying Hawker Harts. He continued his operational training with emphasis on attacks on shipping and instrument flying, gaining his first instrument rating in March 1935. The Squadron seems to have been closely associated with the then embryonic Fleet Air Arm, and took part in several fleet exercises, culminating in participation in the Royal Fleet Review at Spithead in July 1935, during which John took part in the flypast.

It was during this period that John became interested in the sea, and the background knowledge he gained must have served him well during the epic escape from Java which is described later in this book. The young Plt Offr Jeudwine attended courses at the Royal Naval Air Base Gosport, and on board the Aircraft Carrier H.M.S."Courageous", where he learned how to make deck landings and to fly float planes such as the versatile Fairy 111F. In May 1935 he qualified in deck landings and, after a refresher course in August he was posted to 823 Torpedo, Spotter and Reconnaissance Squadron (TSR) and joined the aircraft carrier H.M.S. " Glorious" in the Mediterranean.

The history and tragic end of HMS "Glorious" is very well documented in John Winton`s book "Carrier Glorious", and chapters 3 and 4 cover the period that John was on board. The ship started life as a light cruiser during the First World War, she and her sister ship "Courageous" were launched in 1916. After the war both ships were laid up in reserve, but with the re-emergence of

Photo: RAF College Cranwell

naval aviation work began in 1924 to convert both ships to aircraft carriers. and "Glorious" was re-commissioned at Devenport in 1930. The next two years saw her alternating between the Mediterranean and home waters, carrying mainly Fairy 111F aircraft. In 1934 she was fitted with a new system of arrester wires, and late in 1935 she took on board nine Nimrod aircraft of 802² Squadron and six Fairy Seals of 823 Squadron. John was amongst the pilots of these aircraft. The Seals were replacements for the Fairy 111Fs and were a naval version of the Fairy Gordon, they had a top speed of 138mph and an endurance of four and a half hours.

The Operational Record Book of 823 (Fleet Air Arm) Squadron is rather fragmented, but John`s name appears quite regularly, sometimes associated with 802 Squadron. In January 1936 H.M.S. "Glorious" entered Alexandria harbour Egypt, and just prior to this event John accompanied a Lieut O.S. Stevenson of 803 Squadron in flying two aircraft to the nearby Aboukir airfield, where they were to be used in night flying and bombing practise.In the same month John appears to have had a minor accident whilst taxying, which delayed his return to the aircraft carrier. Several practise bombing attacks took place in February,including a night attack on Alexandria. At the end of February 1936 the Squadron flew to Amyria to the South West of Alexandria for more bombing practise, John was to visit this airfield again in 1942 whilst commanding No 55 Squadron. In March 1936 the name of Jeudwine appears again in connection with having successfully completed a night deck landing course, and promotion to Fg Offr. Meanwhile the Italian /Abyssinian conflict was taking place, and the British Mediterranean Fleet was on standby for any possible eventuality- a situation well known to today's armed forces who have often to wait for the politicians to make up their minds.In April H.M.S. "Glorious" moved to Malta for a spell in dry dock, but in May the Squadron was back in Alexandria, this time under the command of Lieut E.A. Greenwood. Various minor incidents

Number 12 Squadron 1934
Plt Offr Jeudwine seated one from left
Photo: RAF Museum

are recorded, such as when a dinghy broke loose and wrapped itself around the tailplane of an aircraft flown by a Fg Offr Peacock,-luckily the dinghy disengaged itself when the aircraft was just 30 feet above the water, and the pilot managed to recover.The incident lead to the usual "clanging of stable doors" and all aircraft were checked for safety of the dinghy stowage.

During this time John had been studying French and German and in June he flew to Heliopolis airfield near Cairo, where he took and passed his Second Class French interpreter's examination. Six months later he returned to Cairo to take and pass his German interpreters exam. By this time he was proving to be a first class pilot, and in July he was given the task of demonstrating the new Seal aircraft.

In the late summer of 1936 the main Mediterranean Fleet was helping to evacuate refugees from the Spanish Civil War, but "Glorious" was not directly involved. At that time the carrier was under command of Captain B.A. Frazer OBE ADC, a very famous naval officer who went on to become an Admiral of The Fleet. Captain Frazer established a close rapport with his flyers from both the Royal Navy and Royal Air Force, and the carrier became the first to receive the new Fairy Swordfish aircraft. Once again John was chosen for the special task of demonstrating the new aircraft to some high ranking officers of the Turkish Navy. Captain Frazer put great emphasis on night operations and various systems of subdued lighting were being tried to assist pilots to land safely on carriers at night. Night bombing was often practised and the small island of Filfla off Malta was in regular use as a bombing range.It was about this time that a small bar, known as "Beppo`s" and situated near Hal Far airfield on Malta, was in regular use by John and others when they were ashore. Apparently his name is recorded on the walls along with many other names of RN and RAF personnel.

In March 1937 there was a combined fleet exercise in the Eastern Atlantic, and for "Glorious" this involved many night

Hawker Hart from 12 Squadron 1935

1937 Fleet Review-823 Sqn Fly past "Glorious"
Photos: RAF Museum

11

exercises. In May the ship was back in home waters for the Coronation Review and John was involved in the fly past. After the review the squadron was involved in another exercise in the Western Approaches until July when they returned to Malta. Two months later "Glorious" and her aircraft became involved in the Spanish Civil War and in counter measures against some Italian submarines that Mussolini had lent to the Spanish Nationalist forces. In December 1937 Capt Lister took over command of "Glorious" and for the next 18 months the rapport between sailors and airmen continued to grow; No 823(TSR) Squadron was taken over by Lieut Comd Robin Kilroy. A final entry in the squadron log is of John's promotion to become the O.C. "B" Flight on the 26th August 1938, having gained the rank of Flt Lt in the previous January.

During his time with 823 Squadron John had continued to build up his reputation as a fine athlete, taking part in numerous events and winning several trophies, including a cup for winning the one mile race in 1938.

With the war clouds gathering John was posted back to England in January 1939, and he was sent on leave until April, being nominally on the strength of No 1 Depot at R.A.F. Uxbridge. During his leave someone discovered that he was a qualified interpreter in both German and French and on return from his leave he was sent on a specialised signals course at the No 1 Electrical and Wireless School -I think at that time based at Cranwell. The course was obviously connected with Signals Intelligence, (listening in on enemy communications), and John went on to hold three appointments in Signals Intelligence duties.

At the end of November 1939 John was posted to The Air Ministry to work under the Deputy Director Of Intelligence, or Air Intelligence 1(e) in Whitehall, where he would have been closely associated with Group Capt Blandy, who was the Deputy Director Of Signals Intelligence. Here he was probably helping to control the work of the RAF Signals Stations at Kingsdown, Cheadle and Chicksands, and coordinating their work with that of other intelligence gathering organisations. With the expansion of the "Y" Service, as it was known, and with his previous knowledge of the Middle East and Egypt, he was sent out to Cairo in January 1940, and a month later became a founder member of the AM/WT Unit at Heliopolis, which was housed in the partly finished Desert Museum on the Cairo -Suez road. The building was regarded as the HQ of the RAF "Y" Service in the Middle East and contained Numbers 50 and 53 Wireless Units (RAF) and the Army Signals Intelligence Staff known as GSI(S)b. Also in the same building there was located a unit known as CBME, (Combined Bureau ME) which was really an outstation of the now famous Bletchely Park which was reading the German Enigma signals. John, in the rank of Squadron Leader, became the first OC of the RAF unit, and for the next 18 months he and his staff were responsible to DDI 4 at the Air Ministry in London for the interception and collation of German and Italian signals communications. Information obtained from these signals was passed to the relevant service intelligence staffs who used it to outsmart the enemy and, for example, warn of impending attacks on convoys carrying much needed supplies through "bomb alley" as the Mediterranean was known. By a strange coincidence my brother in law was a Met Officer at Heliopolis at this time and would have been in receipt of the weather information contained in some of the intercepted signals.

On more than one occasion during his time at the AM/WT Station Cairo John demonstrated his calm but forceful nature. Always plagued by blowing sand and winter cold, the museum building proved unsuitable, not only for the delicate "X" Machines, but as regards the general working conditions of the staff, whose exacting intelligence gathering duties required a good environment. In December 1940 the records show that John was chasing requests for oil stoves, and in January 1941, following a violent sand storm, John wrote to the Medical authorities, having previously failed to obtain better working conditions for his staff. Eventually he was asked to produce his plans for the construction of a purpose built unit close to the museum. As usual, wherever he went, John was very keen on sport and physical fitness in his units, and there are letters on file[3] in which he is requesting sports equipment. In April 1941 the unit, which had increased in size by the addition of female civilian and Naval telegraphists, was taken over by Wing Commander Phillips.

In August 1941 John was transferred to the Air HQ Palestine and Transjordan, located in Haifa. Here he was probably engaged in establishing one of the several Wireless Intelligence Units, known for security reasons as Field Units, which were controlled by the main AM/WT unit at the Suez Road site in Egypt. The unit in Palestine monitored signals traffic from the Balkans and Russian front.

It was not until September 1941 that The Air Ministry decided it was time for John to take command of a squadron. He was sent to No 70 Operational Training Unit , which had just moved from Ismailia in Egypt to Nakuru in Kenya .It was here that he came into contact with Eric Wyllie, uncle of John Wyllie DFC who served with John in No 84 Squadron during the Far East saga. Eric Wyllie was an instructor at the OTU and later commanded the air crew pool at Gilgil. At Nakuru John joined a course lasting about 5 weeks, during which he spent some 10 hours flying Oxford trainers then some 30/40 hours on Blenheim light bombers. The records are a little hazy at this point but it seems that he probably joined 10 other crews which were on course number 3. In late October 1941 John was moved up to the Canal Zone of Egypt, to take command, for a short while, of the new airfield at Shandur,[4] at the Southern end of the Great Bitter Lake. At that time Shandur was an administrative base, but the airfield was later to become the home of 70 OTU which was moved back from Kenya, and was also used as a base for converting crews onto the new Baltimore and Boston aircraft which were coming into service.[5] In November

14

John handed over command of Shandur to a Wg Cdr Chadwick and was posted, via the Air HQ Western Desert, to take command of No 84 Blenheim Squadron at Heliopolis. This was really the beginning of his life as a wartime bomber pilot, and leads us to the next phase of his career in the RAF.

Notes.

1.They were -John Beecher, H. Denison, Alan Mills and David Gardiner

2.The Adjutant of 802 Sqn at that time was Flt Lt George Stainsworth of Schneider Trophy fame.

3.PRO Air 29/152

4.. In January 1946 the airfield was taken over by the army, and by early 1947 had become home to a regiment of the Royal Tank Regiment and No 1 Armoured Replacement Group in which the author served as a Lieutenant in charge of a maintenance troop.It is likely therefore that I have sat in the same bar and anti room that John used during his time there.

5. In July 1941 No 223 Squadron, which features later in this story, was acting as an OTU at Shandur converting crews to Maryland medium bombers.

L.L-J

Blenheim Mk IV Light Bomber used by No 84 Squadron on operations in the Middle and Far East 1941/1942

Number 84 Squadron Crest

CHAPTER 2

Sumatra , Java and escape by sea

On the fifth of January 1942, John, with the rank of Wing Commander was appointed Commanding Officer of No 84 Squadron. The squadron crest is a Scorpion above the motto "Scorpiones Pungunt," [Scorpions Sting]. The Scorpion was to play a major part in John's life in the coming months. No 84 Squadron had just been withdrawn from action in the Western Desert prior to its posting to the Far East, re-equipped with Blenheim Mark IV bombers and based temporarily at Heliopolis. A number of the squadron's personnel were approaching the end of their overseas tour and consequently were not sent to the Far East; replacements for these were posted in, some being RAAF crews, most, like their new CO, with little or no combat experience. Squadron strength was 24 aircraft, 33 crews and 484 ground staff.

John came to the position of CO from special duties at Air Headquarters, Libya, where he had been engaged in signals intelligence. In fact, apart from a short time at No 70 OTU during which time he converted on to Blenheims and logged about 70 flying hours, John had not been on flying duties since August 1938, when he left No 823 Squadron on the aircraft carrier HMS "Glorious". Whoever was responsible for his appointment either had considerable foresight and faith in his abilities, or was forced to make such a decision under pressure of war, when the Allies were suffering serious setbacks on all fronts. Even so, it would seem that there were many more suitably qualified candidates. A

17

member of the squadron, David Russell, was later to comment of John; "I recall a quiet, slightly built, gentle looking man who appeared to be the antithesis of his predecessor. Who was this guy Jeudwine anyway? Had he done any ops ? God, he didn't look cavalier, did he ? Didn't bawl breezy instructions like Boyce, didn't swashbuckle. "

Nine days after assuming Command of 84, the squadron commenced its departure for Sumatra, leaving in flights on 14, 15, 16 and 18 January, with Jeudwine, piloting his own aircraft, departing on the 16th. Each aircraft carried, besides its normal three man crew, two ground staff, tools, personal kit, spares and an additional 55 gallon fuel tank giving an all up weight of 14,000 lbs [6352 kgs]   The route was to be Heliopolis- Habbaniya- Bahrein - Sharjah - Karachi -   Allahahad - Calcutta - Toungoo- Rangoon - Longka [Sumatra] Medan and finally to Palembang. The route taken across India varied according to weather conditions. There are theories that the Squadron's original destination was to be Singapore or Butterworth in Malaya but it is evident that after consultation in Rangoon John was directed to Palembang. No maps of Sumatra were available and finally a motoring map of part of the area was found and this had to suffice. Of the 24 aircraft that departed, only 16 finally arrived at Palembang , the remainder having suffered mishaps, one fatally, en route. All credit is due to the aircrews when one considers the task of flying recently overhauled or reconditioned, overloaded aircraft over such demanding and lengthy stages with almost no external navigation aids.

Of the flight out from Egypt, Russell was to say- "The long flight from Heliopolis, euphoric at the start, was gradually transformed into a lesson in disillusion. Everywhere we landed we encountered gloom and despondency. The further we flew from Egypt the more depressing things became. A brief meeting with

18

several awful memsahibs at Karachi provided us with a little light relief. They were so patronisingly upper class, so brassy, so dismissive of anyone below the rank of Squadron Leader, that we found ourselves being quite rude to them. Boyce would have bawled us out like a sergeant major, Jeudwine simply touched my shoulder, and said, *tch, tch, Russell, behave yourself.* A twinkle in his eye [a feature we learned to know and expect] indicated complicity, yet he made his point without eliciting rancour."

John and four other aircraft piloted by Flt Lts J.Wyllie, A.M.Gill and G.W.Milson and Plt Offr B. Fihelly arrived at Palembang airfield, designated P1, on the afternoon of January 23 to find that the Japanese had bombed and strafed the airfield that morning. By 26 January 16 aircraft had arrived, all needing 40 hour inspections after their flight from Egypt. This was the least of his problems.

To fully understand the situation it is appropriate to quote from John's own history of the times. "The plan was that No 84 Squadron should be based at Palembang P1 , with the aircrews and maintenance personnel, with the exception of a small maintenance party, quartered in the town which was some eight miles away from the aerodrome. Accommodation was to be in schools, and the one in which the squadron aircrews lived had been designed for a maximum of forty boarders, including staff. In this were crammed the aircrews of three squadrons and the ground staff of one squadron. Conditions were appalling. Cooking arrangements were inadequate and the only means of getting a meal was to go to an hotel where the prices were exorbitant. Crews slept on mattresses on the ground and it was not possible to rig mosquito nets. Luckily the area was non malarial, but the mosquitos were very troublesome. If anyone was away on a night operation, he would find on his return that his mattress had been taken by someone else and quarrels over sleeping space were frequent. The sanitary

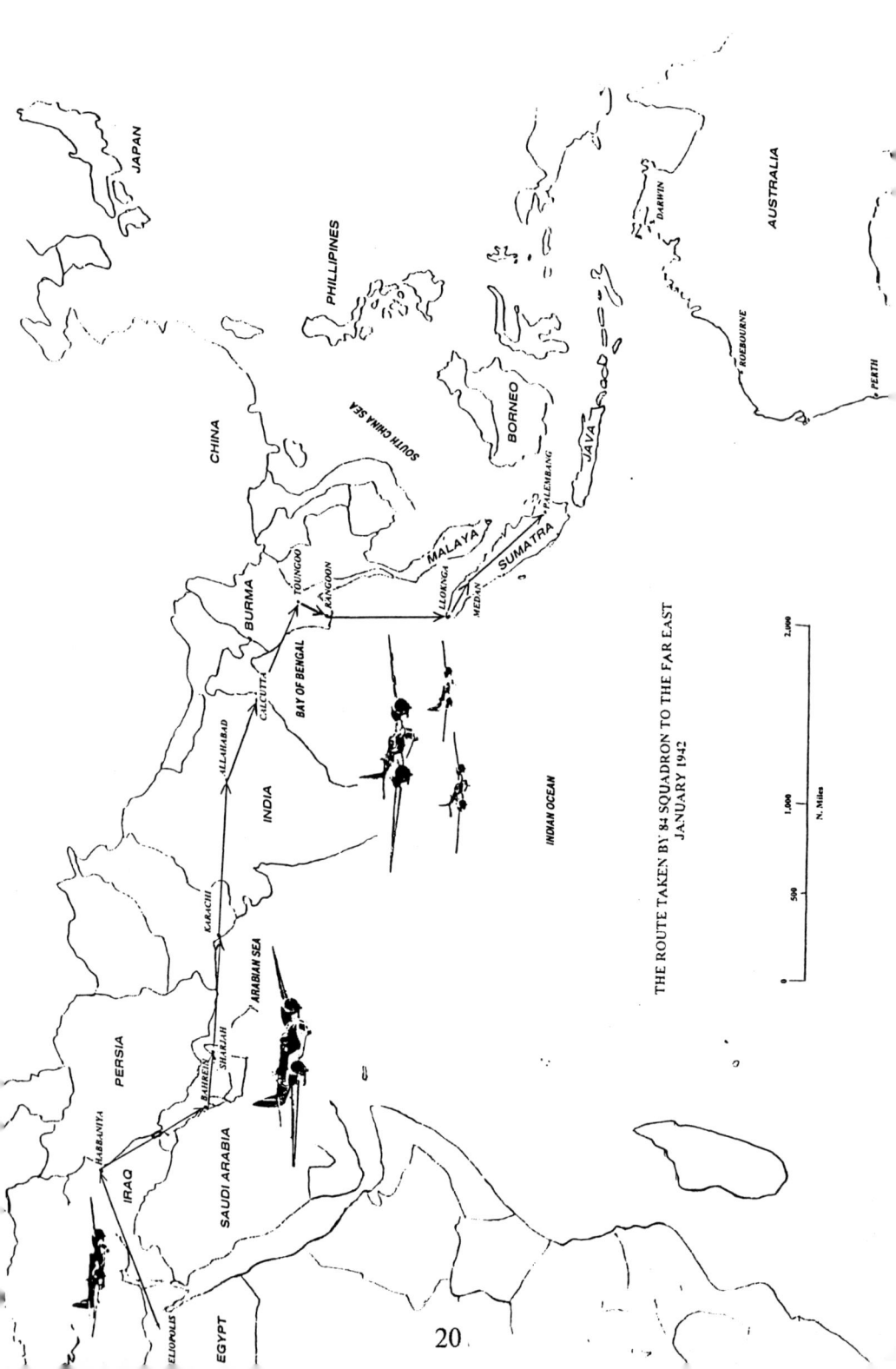

THE ROUTE TAKEN BY 84 SQUADRON TO THE FAR EAST
JANUARY 1942

JAPAN

CHINA

PHILLIPINES

SOUTH CHINA SEA

BURMA
TOUNGOO
RANGOON

BAY OF BENGAL

CALCUTTA

ALLAHABAD

INDIA

KARACHI

PERSIA

IRAQ
HABBANIYA

SHARJAH
BAHREIN

ARABIAN SEA

SAUDI ARABIA

EGYPT
HELIOPOLIS

MALAYA
MEDAN
LLOKNGA

SUMATRA
PALEMBANG

BORNEO

JAVA

INDIAN OCEAN

DARWIN

AUSTRALIA

ROEBOURNE

PERTH

0   500   1,000   2,000
N. Miles

20

arrangements, also inadequate , soon broke down and it was only by good fortune that there was no epidemic. There was however some sickness from gastric complaints."

To add to their difficulties the maintenance facilities and crews were based at another airfield, P2, which was 42 miles away from P1, reached by ferry, as there was no bridge over the river. Here also accommodation was primitive and over two miles from the airfield , the distance being travelled on foot, as there was no transport. Food was scarce and maintenance facilities totally inadequate.

John was highly critical of the RAF organisation, stating that there was a lack of trained support staff, an inability to make decisions due to ignorance of operational need and these factors were largely responsible for the muddles and delays encountered. He wrote... "There were no spares, insufficient refuelling facilities, insufficient armament stocks, an almost complete lack of transport." Little co-operation was received from the other squadrons, most of which were RAAF and he was highly critical of the lack of courtesy, poor discipline and low morale of the Australians. In spite of his feelings he was later to select a predominantly Australian crew for his escape voyage.

This was the situation John found himself in just 21 days after taking command . A newly made up squadron with no time to develop relationships, from desert to tropical jungle, eight aircraft lost or delayed en route, few facilities and the enemy already bombing their base. He was fortunate to have a nucleus of tried and tested men on whom the brunt of operations was to fall and who supported him to the end. One of these was Flight Lieutenant George Milson who had been in the desert with 84 and who arrived at Palembang on the same day as John. Milson was later to write to John's cousin - "During the whole five weeks in the Far East , until things fell apart he [Jeudwine] had no administrative

21

backing, no adjutant or an orderly room, making all his own decisions. Thank goodness they were for the most part the right ones." He goes on- "I did no flying during the two weeks I was in Java, I was off sick with blood poisoning, but became his odd job man, getting to know him very well, realising his problems and the strain he was working under, he was almost working himself into the ground." Milson went on to say that he had served under seven different operational commanders and- "without any hesitation I will say Johnny Jeudwine was by far the best."

To compound their problems the "ground party" consisting of the majority of squadron personnel and equipment was to travel from Egypt by sea on the "Yoma" in conjunction with their opposite numbers from No 211 RAF Squadron The "Yoma" arrived at Oosthaven, a port in southern Sumatra on the day the Japanese dropped parachute troops on the airfield at Palembang. Ultimately the 'Yoma' proved to be the escape vehicle for 132 members of the squadron.

On 25 January, owing to the unserviceability of their own aircraft, John borrowed five aircraft from No 27 Squadron, crewed them with No 84 Squadron personnel, and led an attack on a convoy believed to be landing troops at Endau, North of Singapore. Owing to delays in receiving the signal to attack and a late departure they only reached Singapore after darkness had fallen. In "Bloody Shambles" Part 2 Sgt. Dave Russell, John's air gunner, recalls "Jeudwine ordered Geoff [Sgt Palmer, the navigator] and me to bale out over Sembawang after he had made several awfully ham- fisted attempts to land in the dark. We both refused point blank to do so, and he spent another hair- raising half hour attempting to get down. I suspected that he'd never ever had to land a Blenheim at night but, of course he wasn't going to admit that. His actual landing was atrocious."

On the 30th, flying first to Medan to refuel, John then led six aircraft to bomb the submarine base at Penang. All returned safely to Medan and stayed overnight prior to their return to P2 the next morning. Other targets bombed were at Ipoh and also troop transports off Sumatra. On 2nd February five aircraft, again led by John, took off for Medan to refuel, prior to bombing targets at Songkhla in Siam. In his history, John wrote - "The raids against land targets via Medan were mostly carried out at night and all except those against the Anambas were made via Medan"-. The raids from Medan proved to be very tiring, aircrews had to travel the 42 miles to P2, where they were usually unable to get any lunch, and then be off the ground by 1300hrs so as to arrive at Medan before dusk. After a few hours on the ground, the aircraft would take off on a raid which could be from two to four hours, returning to Medan for a scratch meal and to be off the ground at first light to arrive at P2 where once again there would be no meal and little chance of getting one in town. The day after their return the operation would be repeated. So every other day, crews would fly ten to twelve hours to drop four 250 lb bombs on targets of which they had little or no information. They had one good meal every 48 hours [for which they had to pay] and very little sleep. Yet very few complained.

During the period from 4 to 14 February the squadron carried out continuous raids on various targets, including shipping. During this period a number of machines had been lost through accidents and mechanical failures. Due to the shortage of spares the wrecked aircraft were fair game for the salvaging of parts. On one occasion Sgt. Allan Richardson and WOP/AG Roy Crowe of No 211 RAF Squadron reported: "We were desperate to get new accumulators for one of 211's Blenheims and we knew there was a crashed Blenheim on the field, so we went to retrieve what appeared to be "spare" accumulators from it. We had just got them loose when a Blenheim taxied up beside us and stopped. The pilot stood up through his open hatch and ordered us to replace the accumulators and, although we explained the situation and tried a little logical persuasion, the pilot, who was none other than Wg Cdr Jeudwine, pulled out his revolver and pointed out emphatically that the batteries were the property of 84 Squadron, then threatened he would shoot us to protect his squadron's equipment. We put them back smartly!". [Bloody Shambles, Pt. 2 page 61]

On 14 February a Japanese invasion fleet was reported in the River Moesi leading to Palembang. Nine Blenheims led by John bombed the fleet and then commenced low level strafing attacks. Sgt. Dave Russell, Jeudwine's air gunner reported - "Jeudwine wisely flew along the river bank in order that the turret guns could be used at a favourable angle. I only caught glimpses of upturned yellow faces and rifles pointed in our direction as the Jap soldiers stood bolt upright , disdaining to seek cover as they returned my fire. Jeudwine turned back for another run. In the confusing velocity of low-level attack , I could only direct my fire at an indistinguishable mass of khaki that flashed under me and disappeared under the tailplane. I knew that the plane had been holed in several places , but comforted myself in the knowledge that the enemy were in worse discomfort than myself. Jeudwine embarked on a third run, slowing the engines to the point of stalling, to give me latitude to direct a continuous stream of tracer into the sea of khaki that filled the sights. Once again the Blenheim screamed over the bristling convoy, the pilot banked steeply over the leading barge, then rammed the nose down to make yet another hair-raising, low-level sweep of the river." [Bloody Shambles, Pt. 2 page 112.] Departing on a further attack later in the day, the Blenheims met an oncoming fleet of Japanese aircraft and noticed parachutists dropping behind them. After

Sgts Geoff Palmer-second from left back row- and Dave Russell
front row right, Western Desert 1941 before the move to Sumatra.

Dave Russell aged 78

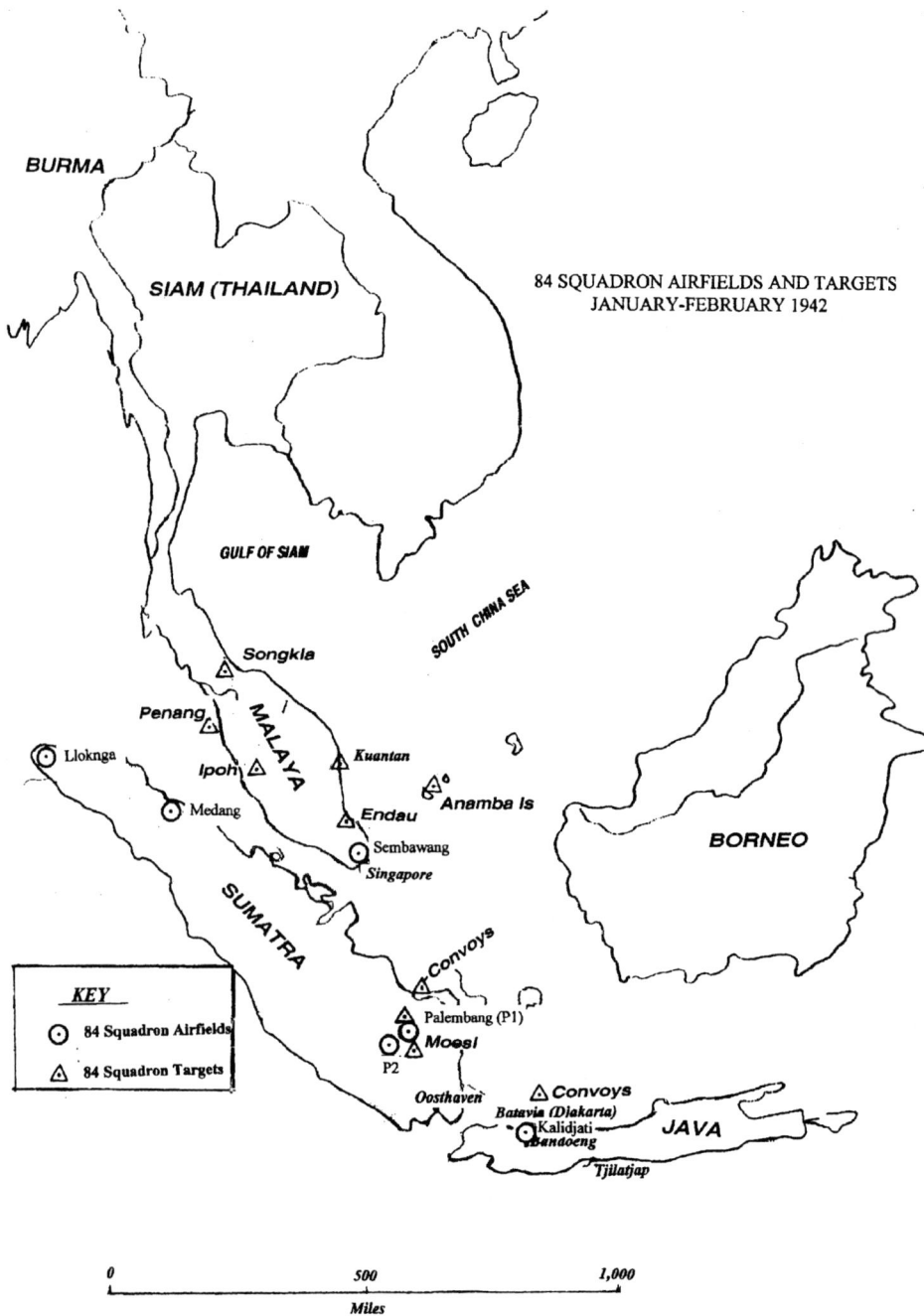

BURMA

SIAM (THAILAND)

84 SQUADRON AIRFIELDS AND TARGETS
JANUARY-FEBRUARY 1942

GULF OF SIAM

SOUTH CHINA SEA

Songkla

Penang

Lloknga

Ipoh

MALAYA

Kuantan

Anamba Is

Medang

Endau

Sembawang

Singapore

BORNEO

SUMATRA

KEY

⊙ 84 Squadron Airfields

△ 84 Squadron Targets

Convoys

Palembang (P1)

Moesi

P2

Oosthaven

Convoys

Batavia (Djakarta)
Kalidjati
Bandoeng

JAVA

Tjilatjap

| 0 | 500 | 1,000 |

Miles

26

bombing the troop transports in the invasion fleet, they returned to P2 and Sgt. Dave Russell comments: "Being turret gunner in Wg Cdr Jeudwine's aircraft, I began to wonder, as the transports got nearer, if there was some form of professional rivalry between the CO and Wg Cdr Bateson of 211 Squadron - had they mutually decided to hit the transports from as low as possible in order to inflict the most damage? It seemed an age before I heard "bombs away" - There was a pause, then the blast of the explosions caused the aircraft to buck and I rose from my saddle , hitting my head on the roof of the turret. I caught a brief glimpse of crowded decks at close range and weapons firing upwards. Before I could depress the twin Brownings to fire, Jeudwine had pulled the aircraft up in a steep climbing turn towards P2, probably as troubled as I was, in case we ran into a crowd of Jap parachutists on their way to capture the airfield. Skirting P1 we could see smoke rising from the burning buildings and collapsed parachutes on the jungle ceiling," ['Scorpions Sting' p 56.] On 15 February Japanese aircraft landed on P1.The evacuation of P2 commenced the same day with Jeudwine ordering Flt Lt Arthur Gill, whose aircraft had been destroyed, to burn all documents and supervise the evacuation of remaining personnel to Oosthaven. Prior to their departure, Gill, with a small group of officers and airmen, made a successful and daring attempt to pick up other squadron personnel and get them over the ferry, where there was considerable congestion and confusion with only one Dutch officer in control.

They finally departed in an overloaded open Ford truck which Gill had commandeered, and they drove through the night in pouring rain for over 300 miles to Oosthaven. There they found the 'Yoma', which had arrived with the ground party from Egypt, about to cast off. They sailed on the 'Yoma' to Batavia, where they picked up additional servicemen and civilians who had escaped from Singapore; then on to India via Ceylon. Of the 605 members of No 84 Squadron who left Egypt, only 132 were to reach India. Arthur Gill was later to be given command of the reformed 84 Squadron after their arrival in India.

Arriving back at P2 after the raids, Jeudwine decided that it would be too dark to fly out that night, so the crews of the remaining Blenheims bedded down under the aircraft, ready to fly out to Kalidjati, about 100 miles from Batavia in Java, at first light. There they joined with Blenheims from Nos 34 and 211 Squadrons, bringing the total number of aircraft up to 29. On the 18th the RAF headquarters announced that all surviving Blenheims would be consolidated into No 84 Squadron under John's command.

From 17 February onwards attacks were launched from Kalidjati on a number of targets, including shipping, oil installations and on their previous base, P1. On the 23rd, John led three aircraft to attack P1 and on the return flight attacked three Jap submarines seen on the surface, one being damaged. While the combined force was fighting back valiantly they were under enormous pressure, as Kalidjati had been bombed by the Japanese on the 22nd and 24th, when 17 bombers escorted by 13 fighters attacked and again on the 25th, when two Blenheims were destroyed out of a force of six being readied for a raid .

Continuous attacks were launched through to the 28th when they attacked a Japanese convoy approaching the coast. For this attack only six aircraft were serviceable and they flew through the night with rotated crews, many of which, including John, flew up to three missions. One of these was Flt Lt John Wyllie who was later awarded the DFC for his successes, sinking and damaging ships in that convoy. "Scorpions Sting" relates that Wyllie, on returning to Kalidjati found that a message had been delivered by dispatch rider to Wg Cdr Jeudwine stating "Maintain maximum dispersal and await further orders". Wyllie

28

realised that John had initiated all operations on his own without instructions from HQ. In a letter to Arthur Gill, dated 14 December 1942, Jeudwine was to describe that night, " All told we put up about 25 sorties. The aircraft were getting fewer and fewer, so as soon as one came down it was re-armed and re-fuelled in a flash and the next crew on the waiting list would take off. The ground crews worked like hell".- By the 1st March only three aircraft were serviceable and the Japs were closing in, Kalidjati being 15 miles forward of the ground defence lines. Orders were given to prepare for evacuation. At 1030 the next morning, Jap tanks arrived on the airfield. There are many stories of heroism during the process of escape; airmen firing sub-machine guns and rifles at the oncoming tanks while, at the same time attempting to blow up the remaining aircraft and stores.

In "Bloody Shambles" Flt Lts Holland and Wyllie described the situation," Three Japanese light armoured cars came half way across the aerodrome and concentrated their fire on us. One of our sergeants rolled over with blood spurting from his neck, a shell splinter had cut his head off. We retaliated with rifle fire which was, of course, little use against armoured cars. We rejoined Jeudwine, who had ordered the evacuation and was standing a little way away beside his car with Flt Lt Owen. As the trucks moved off he indicated that he had three loaded Tommy guns in the car and said " We'll try to draw them off ".We each took a gun and Holland got on one running board of the Chevvy and I got on the other. We each had one arm round the pillars between the open windows. Owen knelt on the back seat of the car and broke the back window with the barrel of his gun. Jeudwine drove and we came back up the road towards the ops hut we had left earlier. It was not an enormously effective ruse but it did draw off two jeep loads of soldiers who chased us for a little

Arthur Gill OBE, DFC. John saved him and his crew from becoming POWs by carrying them out of Singapore in the "well" of his Blenheim. Gill was later to become CO of No 84 Squadron

John Wyllie.Received an immediate award of DFC after attacking a Japanese convoy

way, but they only had rifles-". Thus they escaped and made their way, along with others, to Bandoeng.

Sgt Athelstan [Athel] Snook, who, with his pilot Sgt Alf Longmore and crew member Sgt Phil Corney, all members of No 211 Squadron RAF, had arrived on the "Yoma" with the ground party at Oosthaven, only to be sent to Kalidjati as the Japanese were approaching, describes the situation.- "Finally eight crews, 24 people, were selected and sent to Kalidjati. We were to join 84 Squadron. We ended up at a rather "nice" rubber plantation homestead. As we arrived 24 aircrew, some old friends from Wadi Gozouza, left by the same truck in which we arrived, they were 84 Squadron aircrew being evacuated by sea from Tjilatjap to Ceylon or India. A rather good example of the general madness. Kalidjati aerodrome was about 10 miles from the coast and was perhaps 67 or 70 miles from Batavia.

I have no recollection of any formal induction into the squadron. We just seemed to be absorbed. My first meeting with Wg Cdr Jeudwine occurred when I was inspecting a small circular machine gun pit. My idea was to discover something approaching a " slit trench ". I was with another " hero " inspecting the diminutive ammunition channel and speculating as to whether one could find some protection there. I had my hand on the machine gun and as I leaned down a shadow fell across us. I looked up. It was Wg Cdr Jeudwine. His eyes met mine,- "*Good lad* " he said and passed on. I nearly fainted when I realised he thought I was preparing to defend the aerodrome ALONE !"

The squadron carried out a number of operational flights culminating in a night attack on a Japanese convoy a few miles from Kalidjati. The following morning the enemy arrived by road from their landing point. Some consternation and alarm was apparent amongst the defenders .

31

After reaching Tjilatjap Snook describes the events leading up to their departure- "I recall hearing discussions by several officers in the tugs engine room as to the best way to start the diesel. They might have been chattering about who they should send in next to bat. Well modulated, refined " English " voices were heard discussing the pros and cons of the subject. Every now and then this "drawing room " chat was interrupted by loud bangs, result of the Japs airforces most recent visit. Defeated on the engineering front their eyes turned to the motor boat. A ray of sunshine focussed on the keeling launch, its finest hour was at hand. We lowered two ships lifeboats from a steamer, 28 feet long, clinker built, white with brown trim. Rowed back enthusiastically to the jetty they were tied up on the other side of the launch." One of these lifeboats was to become the HMRAFS "Scorpion." For the time being the war in the air was over for John. In the space of six weeks he had taken command, reformed the squadron, taken it half way around the globe, flown on combat almost daily while organising, leading and motivating the unit in the face of great adversity, only, in spite of his efforts, to ultimately lose almost the entire unit.

On 3 March John received orders from Air Vice-Marshal Maltby, the Air Officer Commanding, that the aircrews of No 84 Squadron, being a reasonably intact group, should travel to the port of   Tjilatjap   on the southern coast of Java to await evacuation. The ground crews, together with the equipment, medical and cypher personnel were to remain at Bandoeng.

David Russell described their arrival in Tjilatjap, " Waves of twenty seven 'Betties' [Japanese bombers] saluted our arrival, wiping out the docks and godowns and the port installations without let or hindrance. The series of large bamboo barracks, each with its long attap sleeping platform, were deserted, but crammed with abandoned equipment, suitcases, kitbags, back

32

packs, wallets of photographs, letters from home, a hopeless jumble indicating a hasty, panic stricken flight. Life had become unreal. We just couldn't understand how people had become so deeply demoralised so swiftly. We took cover in the 'rubber' when the next wave of bombers arrived. Tjilatjap was in flames, the trees were on fire, the billets were burning, we were in the midst of disaster. It soon became obvious that no relief ship would ever hazard approaching the place. When the thunder had ceased we went down to the dockside to view the destruction. Debris and wreckage floated on the calm surface of the estuary, the river reflecting the flames rising from the adjoining buildings. Jeudwine assembled us in reasonable order on the dockside. "Right" he said, and even now he still appeared to be in complete command of himself, "your duty is clear. Wreck everything you can lay your hands on, set fire to the oil storage tanks, wreck the place, then go and find any method of extricating yourself from this mess. It's every man for himself now." Russell goes on to describe the destruction they undertook as a kind of therapy for their anger and disappointment. He continues..." Although 84 had ceased to have any fighting potential, it's aircraft destroyed and its complement of tradesmen scattered all over the island, it's Commander still contrived to maintain his dignity and authority." While some personnel drifted off in search of rescue, the majority elected to take their chances with their squadron commander. They foraged for supplies and loaded these into two ship's lifeboats.

Forty five years later Russell wrote..." I can still conjure up a vivid picture of those old lifeboats low in the water, overloaded with passengers foolishly equipped with kitbags, back packs and suitcases. One guy even carried a portable wireless! Mad ! Jeudwine gave the order to jettison the lot, except for bare essentials. The river estuary was wide and the sea a long distance

33

from our point of departure. Five of our number manned a little launch attached by a rope to the first lifeboat, it being similarly attached to the second. The launch, under full power laboured in great distress, to fulfil its function of towing us to the ocean. We were bound for Australia! The only person who appeared to consider the voyage capable of achievement was Wing Commander Jeudwine, the rest of us were like sheep!. It gradually became apparent that the five guys aboard the launch were in great difficulty, having been breathing fumes from the stricken engine. The tow rope had to be cut and the crew rescued. We were just abreast an island in the mouth of the estuary and, since the second lifeboat was leaking like a sieve, the CO shouted orders for both boats to put in to the shore. Both craft were to be emptied and everyone to assemble on shore. It was quite evident that lifeboat number two was useless. Jeudwine was quick to face reality. In his usual calm way he outlined his plan. One lifeboat with a greatly reduced crew , the second being abandoned, might be able to reach Australia. He'd take only those with a knowledge of sailing, preferably Australians, the remainder would stay on the island with an equitable share of the provisions. Jeudwine promised he would try to send a rescue vessel as soon as he reached Australia in an estimated six weeks."

Athel Snook described his invitation to join the boat party--" We anchored the boat. Swam ashore. Fell asleep. Phil Corney woke me. *The Commanding officer wants to see you* he said, *it looks like you're going.* I looked past him down to where the little white lifeboat lay anchored. It seemed very small against the vastness of the sea which lay beyond the jewel like cove.

We went down to where Wing Commander Jeudwine and others sat by a small fresh water stream. *Do you think you could navigate to Christmas Island* he asked, pointing to a speck on the map. No Sir I said. *Do you think you could navigate to Australia*

34

was his next exciting option. I cheered up at the prospect. No trouble Sir was my confident answer. Just steer South East- you can't miss it   OK he said. I realised the dice had been thrown irrevocably"

Russell continued-"In our innocence Geoff [Sgt Palmer, the third member of Jeudwine's crew] and I thought we were bound to accompany our skipper on his voyage. After all, we had been with him through everything. He took us aside and asked if we knew anything about seamanship. Cursing my Methodist upbringing I replied that I didn't. Geoff was equally honest. I was heartbroken at our rejection, even though I knew that he was right to leave us behind, the trip was risky enough without a couple of dependants clinging to his coat tails.

I spent the rest of the evening swimming to and from the anchored lifeboat, ferrying stuff from the beach. I regarded it as a privilege to carry my pilot's kit on my final swim. The selected crew were all aboard as Jeudwine and I trod water beside the boat, both in tears as we shook hands in farewell. Sitting in the stern, Phil Corney held up a bottle of Veuve Cliquot we'd bought together back in Bandoeng, intending to share it when our relief ship reached Australia. *I'll keep it for when we meet again, Dave* he said. That was the last I ever saw of Wing Commander John Jeudwine or Phil Corney."

Athel Snook, a close friend of Phil Corney and fellow West Australian, was one of those chosen for the voyage, partly due to his knowledge of navigation. Some three years after the event Athel was to write his version of this story and we are indebted to his sister for making his manuscript available. Athel`s description of events leading up to their departure from Java differs little except that he gives insight into the characters of his shipmates and describes their appearance. "Wg Cdr Jeudwine" he writes " is a tall lean man with piercing blue eyes and speaks in a slow

35

English drawl, an excellent officer.   Let me now introduce some of the other members of this enterprise. Here in this twenty eight foot ships lifeboat are twelve men setting out on an adventure with little real knowledge of one anothers true characteristics, with tacit agreement to aid one another in whatever misfortunes may befall them. At the tiller sits the C.O. Jeudwine. He wears a dirty shirt, one of his epaulettes is missing, his feet are bare save for a pair of woolen socks, his long trousers appear to have been slept in more than once. He is in complete command of the ship and personnel, an old Fleet Air Arm man he is one of the very few of us who have any sea knowledge. Sitting next to him up in the stern is Plt Offr Streatfeild, a big man well over six feet, about 33 years old and a permanent man with much experience of flying in all parts of the world. He is dark haired, has a ruddy complexion, his nose is fairly large, his eyes hazel, he speaks with rather a pleasant voice and when he laughs, which is often, the infection of his humour causes others to laugh with him. He is very polite and always defferential when he addresses you. His knowledge of sailing is mostly limited to luxury yachting on the Mediterranean. The young, well built black haired man is Phil Corney. Deep brown eyes, a nose almost aquiline and a fine tan for a complexion somewhat reminiscent of a Red Indian. His is a strong, deep character swept sometimes by moods which make him uneasy to understand fully. Jack Lovegrove is a little fellow, five feet five or six, dark brown curly hair, a sunny smile , blue eyes, good natured. Mort Macdonald, another West Australian, had an excellent flying record, a big happy face surmounting a six foot frame, sandy hair and a somewhat nebulous quality which he refers to as Macdonalds luck.   Of Squadron Leader Passmore I know little save that he was one of the finest men I have had the pleasure of knowing. He was always good humoured throughout all our adversities. he was an excellent pilot and wears the DFC for his

36

gallant work. Plt Offr Sid Turner was trained in Navigation in Canada . He joined Sqn Ldr Passmore and Plt Offr Streatfeild to form a crew . Sid is not a big man, he has light coloured hair, dark eyes and is constrained in his speech. An indominitable will and a first class brain make up the picture. The tall, slim, dark haired, dark eyed man of twentythree or four is Peter Haynes. Son of a well known West Australian Doctor, Peter has a steady wit and is characterised by a slow drawl and happy go lucky ways. An Air Gunner he has seen much war and has managed to surmount all obstacles by a cheery nonchalance. Bill Cosgrove was one of the strangest men I have ever met, a mass of conflicting qualities that would have delighted a psychologist. Consider a tall, excellently built man, fair hair, green eyes, an almost plump face having fairly high cheek bones. He had university brains, an excellent memory, being able to remember the name of every horse that had won the Melbourne Cup from 1920 onwards and could probably inform you of the placegetters in the last ten years. He had played League football for Richmond, a good pilot and knew his work. Yet against this he had absolutely no respect for rank or discipline and was credited with having thrown several Mess Presidents out of their own Mess. He had a remarkably direct manner of speech and a very ready wit. This then was Bill Cosgrove, a hard betting quick thinking man who should have been a fighter pilot. [He later was] George Sayers , who had flown in Abyssinia, the Desert, Greece, Crete, Russia, Java and Sumatra had a most eventful career. Fair haired, blue eyed about twenty six, of medium stature and an intense interest in horse racing and football, he, like Bill Cosgrove came from Melbourne. Alf Longmore was something of a contrast. Dark haired, dark eyed, a South Australian, ex athlete he was of slight built and at the end of our voyage he was showing the signs of malnourishment and exposure. He is a cheery little man , probably the oldest on board being over thirty." Thus Athel

Snook described his shipmates, observations closely parallel to those of Peter Haynes made many years later in 1996.

It is fitting that in spite of David Russell's and Athel Snook's graphic accounts of these events, they are best described in John's own words. His style supports Russel's assessment of his calm nature. Pre-empting the story, John and eleven others finally reached Perth, Western Australia where they were de-briefed by the Intelligence section of Western Area Headquarters.

The following is the narrative, as spoken by Jeudwine and witnessed by Sqn Ldr A. K. Passmore, Fg Offr C. M. Streatfeild and Plt Offr O. S. Turner, who accompanied him on their epic 47 day voyage to Australia.

NARRATIVE.

1. The Situation.

Our story is best told , I think, if I begin with the events on the night of 28 February 1942, when my squadron was operating from an aerodrome in NW Java. This was the beginning of the large scale invasion of Java. We were then informed that Japanese transports were landing troops on the coast NNE of the aerodrome. We bombed enemy transports all that night- the target area was not more than fifty miles distant. All our aircraft returned safely except one, which was driven off by very heavy flak and had to make a forced landing in a rice field. Its crew were saved. Early in the morning the station commander informed me that the Dutch were abandoning the aerodrome and burning all petrol and oil stock. I immediately got in touch with HQ. I was told to remain at the aerodrome, but to disperse and conceal all our aircraft as much as possible and to await further instructions. We did so.

The military defence had completely broken down by this time. There was literally no ground defence at all, with the result that the Japanese surprised us in the morning, arriving with three British made tanks, two armoured cars and about 100 men armed with automatic weapons.

2. The Evacuation.

In view of the uncertainty of the situation, I had arranged the squadron into organised evacuation parties. Each flight knew its transport and what had to be done in the event of an emergency. When the Japanese arrived we had no time to deny them use of our aircraft. Our losses, apart from the aircraft, were 23, a few of whom were certainly prisoners-of-war. We withdrew inland to HQ, but it was soon apparent that we were something of a liability, as we had no aircraft. However, I saw the AOC and he informed me that it had been decided to try to get all surplus personnel out of Java and that, as our Squadron was almost intact from the point of view of personnel, he would try to get us out as a squadron.

I should explain that every man had a rifle, a small amount of ammunition, but no bayonet. We also had a few Tommy guns we had picked up before the evacuation of the aerodrome.

As an instance of the chaotic conditions, I might explain that on the next morning, I learned, quite by accident, that all aircrews including myself, were to go to Tjilatjap, where efforts were to be made to get us off by ship to Colombo.

3. No shipping available.

I got all our aircrews and cars and set off for Tjilatjap. We were told by the embarkation officer on our arrival that there would be no boat that night. The next day Japanese aircraft came over in force and concentrated on the oil dumps, set fire to them and did a lot of damage to the jetty. Two hours after the raid was over, with another officer I set out to try to discover just what damage had been done. We discovered that no effort was being made by the Dutch personnel to salvage shipping in the harbour. I am of the

39

opinion that a lot could have been saved if it had not been left tied up at the jetty. We salvaged one small motor launch.

Two other officers of our party found a Dutch corvette, her fuel tanks full and with ample stores aboard. She had only superficial damage from machine gun bullets, but no damage had been caused to vital parts.Here was a ship that could and would have taken all our aircrew personnel to Australia.

The discovery was reported to our Group Commander, who went to see the Dutch Commander. He sent a message to say he was too busy to see anyone. The next day he tried again. This time the Commander made a variety of excuses, which included that the radio equipment had been damaged by machine-gun fire, that the Dutch themselves were going to use the Corvette and, finally that it had been decided to sink it in the mouth of the harbour. Nothing would move him from this non co-operative attitude. The same afternoon the Dutch began a systematic destruction of everything in the dock area, including fuel stores.

Most of our personnel had been employed trying to salvage petrol from the Dutch demolition parties. I had been sent by the Group Captain to try to discover whether, by chance, any ships had been abandoned on the coast. I could not discover any. When I returned, however, I found that orders had been given for all personnel to go inland to another town.

4. Escape if possible.

Some sixty of my squadron had remained at Tjilatjap and the Group Captain told me that, if we could make a getaway, we could do so. I set a number of my squadron to salvage all the food supplies they could and another party, headed by myself, went round the harbour looking for some likely craft. All we could find were two ships lifeboats- 30 feet long- without auxiliary engines- which we managed to salvage from a KPM liner. All this time huge fires were raging in and around the harbour, mighty clouds of black smoke rising high in the sky.

We got our two lifeboats to the jetty, then divided up our personnel. We still had the motor launch we had salvaged and into this we put five men, the other boats taking thirty each. The idea was to let the launch tow both boats as far as she could with her available petrol, then jettison her, the five men forming her crew being divided between the two lifeboats.

As we were working, one of my officers dashed up to say that a Dutchman had just informed him that the Japanese were landing at the other end of the harbour. He had barely finished speaking when there were loud explosions. He explained that the Dutch were blowing up bridges connecting the harbour and docks area with the mainland, I found out a little later that there was no truth in the statement about the Japanese, and I am convinced this was a deliberate fifth column effort on the part of our Dutch informant.

Our strength was now 65 officers and men, all aircrew with the exception of a few aircraftmen. We had salvaged a ships sextant, two compasses [one an aircraft compass which proved by far the most valuable] a 1/15,000,000. map, but no proper charts.

Our food supplies consisted of biscuit [ration and ships], bully beef in 6 pound tins, meat and vegetable in tins, a little camp pie, some canned tomatoes, tins of plums, beans and two tins of jam, Nestle's and Libby's milk, 6 pots of honey, 24 jars of fish paste, 48 cans of sardines, six bottles of whisky, four bottles of brandy, and some cocoa. [Author's note: John made no mention of the 980 cans of American Pabst beer "liberated" by Sgt Peter Haynes. More of this later!] We also had two Tommy cookers and after two severe storms through which we later passed we were able to make steaming cups of cocoa for all of the party who finally made the trip. We also had three ships beakers of water, one

41

full, the others about two-thirds full. In addition there were six 12 gallon [50 litre] casks which were also full.

We started out from Tjilatjap shortly before 11 pm on the night of 6 March 1942. We soon found that the motor launch would not tow the lifeboats and we could not steer a course. Then we tried our sail, but owing to the overloaded state of the boats again we were unsuccessful. So we decided to return to a cove to the south of the mouth of the river which leads to the harbour at Tjilatjap.

Only two of us, Plt Offr Streatfeild and myself, had ever done any sailing at all. He was in charge of one lifeboat, while I had charge of the other. I decided to anchor off the cove, which had a rocky approach. Streatfeild however thought he could find a passage. His boat was holed and the motor launch wrecked. There were, however, no casualties and we set to work to salvage all the stores and get them ashore. Then we decided to hold a conference to consider our next move.

At this point it is appropriate to interrupt John's narrative and quote George Milson's account of these events. He writes- "We left Tjilatjap about midnight in two lifeboats found on a KPM ship found in the harbour, being towed by a motor-boat. There were five of us in the motor boat and 30 in each of the lifeboats, plus some food and drink; the idea being to run the motor-boat until we ran out of fuel and then sail. After about two hours, the engine gave up the ghost and when the sails were tried, it was found that the boats were overloaded and could not be sailed. One of the lifeboats took us in tow with oars towards a bit of beach on the island of Noesa Kembangan, a small island off Java. The surf caught the motor-boat and the lifeboat, bumped them on some rocks and knocked the bottoms out. We swam ashore, the CO anchoring his boat off, and we salvaged all the food from the two wrecks.

Mid afternoon the CO woke me to tell me that he had decided to set off with a total crew of twelve,- splitting the food and drink down the middle. We who were left were to try and hang on for two months, in which time he expected to get to Australia and send something to get us off. We stayed for six weeks, eventually being found by some Dutch men, who took us along to a jail on the island which was holding convicts for murder etc. They gave us a meal and then handed us to the 'Nips' on the mainland, to be followed by three and a half years of POW life."
The narrative continues-

We decided that one boat should try to make the trip to Australia as there seemed to be a reasonable chance of doing so. Next came the task of picking a crew, which was not so difficult as might be thought. Not more than eight men of the thirty in each lifeboat had escaped violent sea sickness the night before when we attempted the tow, and there was not much point in choosing men who, if the lot fell on them, might for reasons of health be unfit for the trip. Hence we decided to pick the crew as we would have selected crews for an air operation.

As I have explained, Plt Offr Streatfeild and myself were the only members of the party who had experience of handling a boat. [Author's note. This was later challenged by two of the crew.] Plt Offr Turner was our only navigation officer who had experience of astro navigation, Sqn Ldr Passmore was selected because he was the pilot of the crew formed by Plt Offr Streatfeild and Plt Offr Turner and therefore that was one complete crew; and, in addition, I felt that I required a senior officer with me to act as my second-in-command.

It was quickly decided that Australian members of the party should be given first refusal to make the trip and these were selected for their stamina, morale and initiative. It is pleasing to be able to state that, after six and a half weeks of trial, I would not,

43

if the opportunity again occurred, alter one of my crew. They were magnificent. Naturally, we had our disagreements- our accommodation was so taxed that this was unavoidable but in the main we remained staunch friends in adversity.

5. The Departure.

Our crew completed we set off again just as dusk came on 7 March. The only signs of enemy activity we had seen during our stay in the cove had been the appearance of a Navy "O" fighter which came over on the morning of that day, made several circuits of Tjilatjap, and then disappeared. Whether the pilot saw us I do not know. Certainly he displayed no interest in us. So far as the harbour and town were concerned, they were still an inferno.

The 7th of March was a Saturday. All next day we were becalmed off the coast. Next day the calm continued until about 2.30pm when a gentle breeze sprang up and we had just begun to move when, to our horror, about a mile astern of us a Japanese submarine suddenly surfaced. Her conning tower opened and we saw an officer scrutinising us through glasses. Beside him stood another man, probably the coxswain. There was one rating forward at the breach of a six pounder gun and another standing by a machine gun which, however, was pointing to the sky. The submarine was about 600 to 800 tons and gave the impression of having been at sea for a long time. Her paint had flaked off badly and she looked dirty and dingy. But her number, in the shape of an inverted letter "Y " with the figures 56 stood out very clearly on the side of her conning tower.

The submarine approached to within fifty to one hundred yards of us, made a half circle, all the time we were being watched by the officer with the glasses, then she disappeared slowly to the east, still on the surface. I do not have to emphasise our reaction. [Author's note. In the ships daily log Jeudwine wrote that when the submarine appeared they all had a can of beer, the idea being that if the submarine was Japanese they would all be shot; if it was American it would be "dry" !]

The breeze continued to hold and finally freshen. We set off, beating the whole way because of head winds, steering South East.

6. Australians good work.

I want to pay particular tribute to the work of three of the RAAF personnel on board. Our rudder had been damaged when we salvaged the lifeboat and, on the second day out, it broke away completely. It would have been impossible to hold our ship on our long voyage on an oar and I say unhesitatingly that if it had not been mended we should never have survived.

Sgts. Corney and Lovegrove appointed themselves our shipwrights and, after at least three days work they managed to effect a repair with bits of wire from Bully Beef tins and bits of salvage aboard. This was accomplished in bad weather and was a remarkably fine piece of work. Sgt. Snook is also to be highly commended for his assistance in navigation.

I appointed Sqn Ldr Passmore as our purser and he fixed the following ration scale, allowing for what we hoped would be a 30 day trip. Actually we had not made allowance for calms, more of which will be told later. A day's ration for every man aboard consisted of:-

9 oz [253 gms] of bully beef or camp pie. Six ration biscuits. A spoonful of beans or tomatoes. A little fish paste. Occasional issue of canned plums. About half a pint [350 ml] of water. One 12oz [300ml] can of beer. We found that seawater affected the tinned fruit and we had to finish it off quickly.

7. Saturday Naval Nights.

To help maintain morale I instituted the Navy custom of "Saturday night at sea". We gave all hands an extra ration of beer and we opened a bottle of whisky. We all had a tot to drink the "King's Health" as well as the old navy toast of " Sweethearts and

45

Wives [may they never meet] "As is also the navy custom we called upon the youngest member of the crew to reply to the toast. The first time it fell on Sgt Snook he informed us he was no speaker. We discovered that for ourselves shortly after.

We divided our watches as follows- I took Port watch and Plt Offr Streatfeild Starboard watch. At first Plt Offr Streatfeild and I did all the steering, but when calmer weather came we taught other members of the crew to handle the boat, but we made a point of taking over when anything like bad weather threatened a bad sea. For covering we each had one blanket. There were several ground sheets and one or two gas capes. Our main problem was space, and sleeping meant just lying down where any sort of room could be found.

8. Water problem.

I have already stated that when we started we had ample water supplies. But after the first bad storm we encountered, we discovered that a tap on one of the beakers had become loose and most of the content lost, while another barrel's contents were lost when the barrel turned over. In addition three other casks became contaminated with sea water and had to be jettisoned. The water problem, therefore, was a serious one. Then we ran into another fierce tropical storm and that downpour undoubtedly saved our lives, for we were able to catch enough water, using our waterproof sheets and anti-gas capes, to fill our water barrels completely. In passing, we found that with our crew of twelve, rationed as I have explained, a ship's beaker lasted us about fourteen days.

During that terrific storm our rudder broke loose again. Once more Sgts. Corney and Lovegrove set to work and, after 36 hours' work, they managed, by using a piece of metal which they beat out with all sorts of makeshift tools, to get it in good order. Another excellent piece of work.

9. Becalmed.

Then we ran into a calm and, for six days we lay on a glass-like sea. We rigged up an awning-part of the ship's equipment- and this helped a bit, for the heat was terrific. Our biggest problem during those six days was to keep ourselves amused and good tempered. So I organised a series of "mental tests" such as the longest list of film stars whose name began with the letter "S", the biggest list of objects named in a certain number of minutes; competitions between the forecastle and the quarterdeck.

10. The inquisitive whale.

After the sixth day a breeze sprang up and once again there was plenty to keep us occupied during our respective watches. We had seen whales in the distance, blowing, but had thought little or nothing of them, when about a month after we had started our voyage, we received possibly the worst fright of our trip. A mighty whale surfaced about 200 yards astern of us and then began to overtake us rapidly. It eventually came right alongside the boat, its great tail beneath us, and then in some extraordinary way it's head appeared above the water. I am certain it was not more than three feet from us and this awful looking monster remained there apparently staring at us for what seemed a lifetime. We all kept perfectly still. A flick of that tail and that would have been the end of us, lifeboat and all, then, as suddenly as it had appeared, it suddenly submerged and we never saw it or any of its fellows again.

11. Frazer Island.

On the early morning of 16 April Sgt. Corney, who was on watch, declared that he was positive he had smelled Spinifex. [a native Australian shrub]. We had also seen lots of seaweed and, checking up, I reckoned that we should be about fifty miles off Roebourne. Then to my horror, when sunset came and I checked my watch, I realised that it had lost and was possibly forty minutes slow and we might be as much as six hundred miles off the coast. I announced this to my crew on the morning of 17 April and you can guess their feelings. We promptly cut our rations down and decided to do without a midday meal. That night however, and on the following day we began to see unmistakable signs of land again. Two butterflies, ordinary flies, seaweed and a species of jellyfish we had never seen before.

On 19 April, at night we heard the sound of an engine, not loud enough to be an aircraft engine but possibly a small motor boat, but although we lit a red flare we got no response. Then, at 0230 WST we touched land at Frazer Island. We lay offshore until daylight and then went ashore for breakfast. After 44 days at sea we were like drunken men at first. Our legs would not support us and most of us promptly fell over. It did not take long, however, to accustom ourselves to dry land, but, about 10.30am, we started off again. About 3.30 pm that afternoon we sighted a flying-boat going SW. It was about ten miles off. We waved and flashed mirrors but it took no notice. It later transpired that the pilot had seen us, but thought we were a pearling lugger and had not taken any notice of us. Next day we touched another Islet which we named Butterfish Islet because, after we landed, we used some hooks we had aboard and parachute thread to catch our first fish meal for weeks. It was excellent and did us all good.

We set sail again, bearing SE, and at approximately 3 pm that afternoon we saw another flying-boat coming towards us. We raised a pyjama jacket on the signal halyard as a signal of distress and the flying boat alighted. We were signalled by semaphore asking all about us, so I swam over to the boat and explained. The pilot was very wary and would not allow me to go on board, quite rightly I thought afterwards, if not at the time. Eventually we made them understand who we were and they agreed to take six of us. Only three volunteered to go, however.

The remainder of us resumed our voyage, but the following day the flying boat reappeared again at about 1pm and said orders had been received that we were to be taken on board. We took on board such of our belongings as were serviceable and turned the lifeboat adrift. Only one thing we now regret, in the excitement of the evacuation of the boat, we left behind in the forward locker the 84 Squadron shield which consists of a Scorpion and a Latin motto. We shall all be immensely grateful if when the lifeboat drifts ashore, as it must, whoever finds the shield will return it to us as it has been with us through desert warfare and so to Australia.

12. Hospitality.

I should like on behalf of my crew to pay tribute to the extreme kindness with which we were received by the U.S. navy personnel aboard the USS Childs and by the crew of the Catalina. They could not do enough for us and we are correspondingly grateful to them.

In conclusion, our health was remarkably good. We had no fever, but we did suffer from ulcers and abrasions, we also had eye trouble through exposure to sea and sun.

Chills we doctored with Aspirin and Quinine, of which we had a small supply. We made a point of swimming over the side daily, six of us going into the water while the remainder kept watch for sharks.

END OF NARRATIVE.

This verbal account of the journey given by John is a very matter of fact and laconic description of a voyage fraught with danger, tension, doubt and discomfort and makes little or no mention of the excellent seamanship and boat handling skills displayed. While the narrative in itself makes interesting reading, it is the actual ship's log, recording daily events, which reveals the true drama of the passage. Even this at times glosses over the severity of the weather conditions which caused extreme discomfort and danger, as is the case of the log entries for Sunday 22 March and Saturday 11 April.

The log of HMRAF Ship " Scorpion ", reproduced in total in Appendix 1 is the official record of the events which took place over the forty seven days of the voyage They calculated that the nearest point on the Australian coast was Roebourne, 950 nautical miles away, with Port Hedland and Onslow a little further away to the West and East of the aiming point. A Bartholomew's school atlas [the recipient of much abuse later] showed favourable winds and currents and they calculated a voyage of 16 days duration, but they allowed for double that time. Navigational aids were a sextant, a 1/15,000,000 Mercator's projection of the world and a Nautical Almanac giving declension tables and time apparent noon.

The crew consisted of:-

Wing Commander J.R. Jeudwine	RAF	Captain
Squadron Leader A.K. Passmore	RAF	2i/c/Purser
Fying Officer C.P.L. Streatfeild	RAF	1st Lt and
		2nd Healmsman
Pilot Officer S.G. Turner	RAF	Navigator
Pilot Officer M.S. Macdonald	RAAF	
Sgt G.W. Sayer	RAAF	
Sgt. W.N. Cosgrove	RAAF	
Sgt. A. Longmore	RAAF	
Sgt. J. Lovegrove	RAAF	
Sgt. A.C.E. Snook	RAAF	
Sgt. P.M. Corney	RAAF	
Sgt P.Haynes	RAAF	

Passmore was selected as he was the next senior officer. Turner was the only one with astral navigation skills and with Streatfeild they were a complete aircrew. In addition Streatfeild, along with John, had some sailing experience. The other crew members, all Australians were selected for their apparent lack of sea sickness, their initiative and courage and because John felt that Australians should have first chance to reach their homeland.

The crew of the "Scorpion"

Back row L to R. Cosgrove, McDonald, **Jeudwine**, Streatfeild

Middle row L to R. Corney, Passmore, Haynes, Turner,

Front row L to R. Lovegrove, Sayer, Snook, Longmore

Photo via Robert and Misaka Piper, Australia

51

From a painting of the "Scorpion" by Athel Snook in 1984

The copy of the Scorpion's log reproduced in the Appendix was sent to Sqn Ldr Arthur Gill who was then commanding the re-formed 84 Squadron in India. John's history of the events from departure from Egypt to his arrival in Australia from which much of this story is taken was included. John wrote to Gill six months after his escape as follows;

Wing Commander J.R. Jeudwine
No 55Squadron,
RAF ME.

September 7th 1942

Dear Gill,

I am sending you four copies of the Squadron history from the time we left Heliopolis in January until we ceased to be a squadron in March this year. I have written the history in narrative form from my own personal memories and unfortunately I am not able to give details of names or numbers of crew participating in various raids.

However it may be of interest to you to know what happened to the chaps after we were sent to Java while you were being sent off to India. I am also sending you four copies of "The Scorpion" It is not as well produced as I had hoped. One member of the crew was a very clever cartoonist and he produced several sketches to illustrate the log, but unfortunately they never reached me.[1]

However, here it is in its bare form. It might cause you some laughter, it certainly caused us very little at the time, but it is a plain statement of facts. You might like to send a copy to Ashmole if he is still in India.

There is no copyright, but I do reserve the right of making it into a book when the shouting and the tumult has died.[2]

Yours sincerely

J.R. Jeudwine

Authors notes.
1. This was Athel Snook, who died in Perth WA on 4 December 1991. .
2. Note. Flt Lt. Ashmole escaped from P1 with Gill and reached India on the "Yoma".

John wrote to Gill again on 14 December 1942 , a letter which reveals his concern for the squadron members who were left behind in Java......" I think the worst tragedy of the whole show was that Milson and the other crews whom we left on the island off Tjilatjap had gone when help reached them. I often wonder what happened to them . Whatever happened, the fact that they were not there when the submarine called for them takes away any satisfaction I may have felt on making the boat trip successfully". He continues.... " I had a letter from Keith Passmore the other day, he is at a 'Wimpy' [Wellington bomber] OTU, 'Stretty' Streatfeild is at Bicester and Syd Turner, I believe, is up in Yorkshire. They hope to resurrect *The Queen* next year."
The *Queen* was Keith Passmore's aircraft, all of which were named "Queen of Shaibah" and the women's garters flown from the mast of "Scorpion" usually accompanied Passmore on operational flights, hooked over the pitot- head of his aircraft. After their return to England, the RAF members of the 'Scorpion's' crew presented John with a silver mug, bearing the inscription "Up the Queen".
John continues in his lengthy [8 page] letter to Gill , advising that he has left No 55 Squadron and had been posted to Headquarters, Middle East as a staff officer or 'gaberdine swine', as he puts it. After praising the achievements of No 55 Squadron for their pursuit of the war against the Germans in the Western Desert he reveals.....' I'm afraid I did not see quite eye-to-eye with my superiors about the way in which a squadron should be run. I

maintained that it should be led, while they maintained it should be driven, and well you 'can't fart against thunder'. If there is any advice I can give you now that you are a squadron commander yourself, which is pure presumption on my part, is that it is far better to lead than to drive, even though it does cost you your job. You get far more out of the men that way. I always assume that a person will do his best and, until he shows that he cannot be trusted to do his work, I try to treat him like a human being. If he won't try I then get extremely rude and have him posted; and I found that worked out all right, although, as I said, I eventually got posted myself. I was told I was too kind-hearted, not ruthless enough! "

For the final word of John's Far East experiences Air Ministry Bulletin No. 8709 of 15 December 1942 is appropriate.
Royal Air Force Awards No. 462.
Wing Commander John Raymond Jeudwine, No, 84 Squadron.
O.B.E.
When the order was given for evacuation at Bandoeng, the squadron aircrews proceeded to Tjilatjap and awaited embarkation. Wing Commander Jeudwine , undaunted by the non-appearance of the ship detailed, immediately set to work to save as many of his squadron as possible from falling into the hands of the Japanese. He refused to believe that all channels of escape were closed. Wing Commander Jeudwine set out in a car to search the neighbouring coast and ports for a suitable craft. Two lifeboats were discovered on the upper deck of a bombed ship, which he decided to use as a last resort. During his absence, a party, detailed by him , set out to procure the necessary provisions and navigational equipment for the voyage. Wing Commander Jeudwine, being unable to find any other suitable craft, decided to use the lifeboats and ordered them to be lowered and made ready.

During the voyage his ingenuity and sound seamanship enabled the craft to be kept seaworthy in spite of recurring mishaps to the boat and its gear. Many repairs to the rudder were carried out as a result of his resourcefulness and refusal to accept defeat. The repairs necessitated working overboard and Jeudwine insisted on sharing the risks in a shark-infested sea. His continued cheerfulness, courage and ability to bolster up morale were an inspiration to the whole crew.

With this citation Wing Commander John Raymond Jeudwine was made an Officer of the Most Excellent Order of the British Empire.

Authors note on Chapter 2.

Having been born nineteen years after John my recollection of World War Two is that of a ten year old, living in South Africa and remote from the hardships of war, but not untouched by its tragedies. I lost my elder brother Harold in the battle for Crete in May 1941. He was six months older than John. Harold was in 14 Squadron RAF and met John in Egypt only a few months before his death. In his diary Harold wrote of his excitement at meeting his English cousin John for the first time and a photograph of John taken at that meeting is in his photograph album.

I recall being told by my father that his nephew Raymond [as he called John] had escaped from the Japanese by sailing a small boat to Australia. The magnitude of this feat was, I think, not comprehended by any of us at the time. Later my family received the news that John had been killed.

Many years later, after moving to Australia I received a tape recording of a radio drama entitled " A School Map Odyssey " This had been recorded in the late 1950's or early 60's and featured the voyage of the "Scorpion " The tape had been broadcast by a West Australian radio station and most of the material had been contributed by Athel Snook, a crew member of the "Scorpion". Regrettably the recording deteriorated over the years and was lost.

The story of the "Scorpion" made a lasting impression on me and when, about 1995, I started detailed research into the life of family members I advertised in the Royal Air Force journal in an attempt to trace personnel who had served with John. The flood of correspondence not only alerted me to John's incredible strength of character, interesting personality and leadership style but also to his remarkable achievements as a pilot and leader.

Research led me to Peter Haynes OBE, JP, sole living survivor of the voyage of the "Scorpion" and eyewitness to John's role as commander during the voyage. I had the pleasure of spending two days with Peter and his wife Jean in January 1997 and for his contribution my heartfelt thanks. Special thanks to Wing Commander Arthur Gill OBE DFC AE RAF Retd. who contributed substantial first hand observations and for his permission to quote John's personal letters to him.

Special thanks also to David Russell MBE, who, as John's rear gunner was in the thick of it all. David's vividly descriptive letters filled with tragedy and humour made me think that I had known John in real life. David's ability to write of his years in captivity and the hardships suffered with humour and insight are a tribute to character and inner strength.

After his escape to Australia John wrote in a letter to Arthur Gill that he hoped to write his story after the war. That was not to be. I believe that his self effacing style and modesty would not have permitted him to tell of his exploits as they should be told. I hope this book does justice to a man who served his cause nobly and who touched the life of many of his fellow men.

Geoffrey S. Jeudwine
Gold Coast, Queensland ,Australia.   May 1999

Reminiscences: Athel Snook (right), Peter Haynes and John
Lovegrove discuss their boat trip some 50 years after the event.

Photo: Peter Haynes

This page deliberately left blank

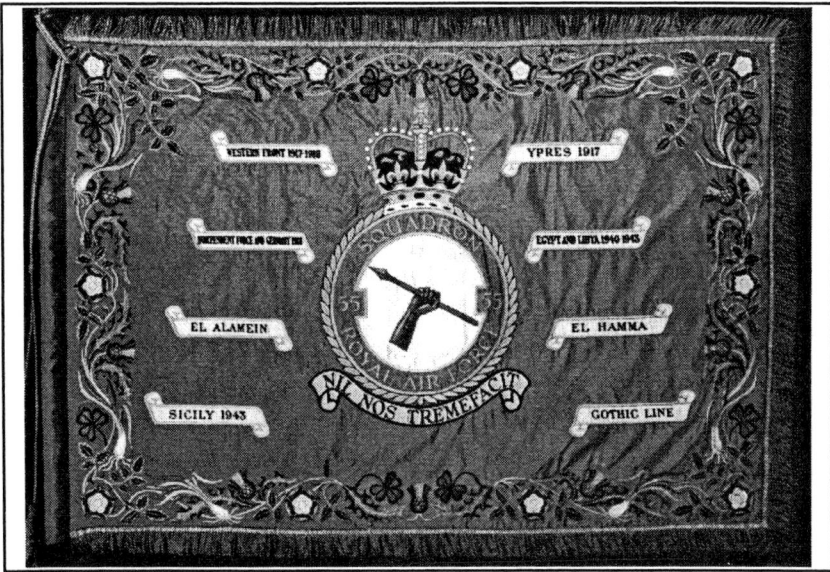

Number 55 Squadron Standard with crest and Battle Honours
Egypt and Lybia 1940-1943 and El Alamein

CHAPTER 3

Back to the Middle East

At the beginning of July 1942, some ten weeks after reaching Australia in "The Scorpion" John said goodbye to his Australian hosts and embarked on a slow steamer bound for India.After seventeen nail biting days, during which he was in constant danger from a Japanese raider, he reached Colombo , where, as luck would have it, he met a Fleet Air Arm pilot that he knew from his days in the Mediterranean. His friend managed to get him into an aircraft carrier bound for Mombassa, from whence he talked his way onto a flying boat on route to Egypt.After some delay in Khartoum, John finally reported to the Headquarters of the Middle East Air Force in Cairo, retaining his temporary rank of Wing Commander. Eager to get back to the war, and away from the "Penguin House" as he called the Headquarters, he joined No 55 Squadron at Landing Ground 207 on the Cairo -Ismailia road, and became their new Commanding Officer, taking over from Wing Commander Ford-Kelin at the end of July.

British fortunes in the desert war had gone through a bad patch since John left the area in the previous January.Shortly after his departure for the Far East, Rommel's Africa Corps opened up a new offensive in the Western Desert and recaptured Benghazi.Checked by the 8th Army on the Gazala line in February, both sides had then made use of a period of relative quiet to reinforce and re-supply their armies. While this was taking place there was a great scare that the Germans intended to capture Malta by using paratroops, but this came to nothing,-probably because of the German need to withdraw some Luftwaffe units to the Russian front.

On the 26th May 1942 Rommel launched a new attack against the Gazala line, some 30 miles West of Tobruk, turning the British

Southern flank, but encountered heavy resistance which caused him to set up temporary defensive positions and the infamous tank trap which became known as the "Cauldron",only ten miles West of the important port of Tobruk.Two previous attempts by the 8th Army to destroy the enemy forces in the "Cauldron" had failed as they came up against the German dual purpose 88mm guns, losing many tanks in the process. Rommel then launched a new attack, and by the 13th June the British were pulling back once again. On the 21st Rommel entered Tobruk, gaining large amounts of equipment and stores.

In spite of a change in command the British continued to retreat during June, losing more troops and much needed supplies, and by the time John returned to the Middle East they were setting up their defensive positions at Alamein, and General Montgomery was taking over command of the 8th Army. Thus it was against this background that John rejoined the war, and began flying in No 55 Squadron's newly acquired A30s (Baltimore) twin engined bombers. He was to leave the squadron in November during the second phase of the now famous Battle of Alamein. Quite why he left after such a comparatively short period in command is not very clear, but in a private letter to Wing Commander Gill, written while temporarily back at the HQ RAF Middle East, he indicates that he did not always see "eye to eye" with his superiors over the handling of 55 Squadron,-being too soft on them. However the views of his contemporaries in the squadron suggest that he was a fine Commanding Officer, and that he had greatly improved their morale and efficiency during his short stay, always leading rather than driving, and of course taking his full share of operational sorties,which are now summarised.

His first operation with No 55 Squadron was from Landing Ground "Y", a satellite of LG 207.On the 25th July, just four days after taking command, he flew in Baltimore AG 814 to bomb a concentration of enemy motor transport near Deu Abayd.

A Baltimore coming in to land, probably at LG86, over the
living area of No 55 Squadron, football match in progress in the
foreground.

Camp life. Sgt Ron Fuller with his pilot, in trousers,and the
two Australian WOP/AGs. John would not have objected to the
departure from dress regulations, preferring to concentrate
on training and keeping casualties to a minimum. "Brew tin"
bottom left

His crew comprised Fg Offr Hornby, Flt Sgt Perkins and Plt Offr Scillicorn, a crew he kept for most of his operational flights with this squadron. Five other aircraft of 55 Squadron were on the raid, piloted by Sqn Ldr Tony Plinston, Flt Sgt Baker, Flt Sgt Payne, Sgt Sage and Sgt Howard. The squadron was in company with other aircraft from No 223 Squadron.With the same aircraft and crew he attacked Al Daba railway station on the 4th and 5th August. On the 9th August he changed aircraft to Baltimore AG 830, but with the same crew bombed Al Daba again.On the 14th August , still in AG 830 the target changed to a transport column near Landing Ground 18, north of Fuka. John was continually on operations throughout the summer and autumn of 1942, operating against Rommel's Africa Corps, the targets being mostly concentrations of tanks and motor transports in the coastal strip between Alamein and Halfaya with which Rommel was hoping to break through the Alamein line. Most of the attacks were made in the morning using 250 or 500lb bombs. Somedays the crews would carry out two or more operations in one day, one before and one after midday, with the squadron mounting as many as seven in one day. A full summary of John`s participation in all this is given at the end of this chapter.

The attacks were often made in the company of other squadrons, notably No 223 RAF, also equipped with Baltimores, 82 and 83 of the USAMEAF (B25 Mitchells)[1]and Nos 12, 24 and 434 Boston squadrons of the South African Air Force, in fact in the early days, after converting to Baltimores, Tony Plinston`s flight was under the control of 223 Squadron which was based just South of Landing Ground 99 on the Alexandria -Cairo road.The Squadron was under the operational control of No 232 Wing which was part of 201 Group, the Headquarters of which was in Alexandria.

The normal pattern for an attack, as described by Tony Plinston and Ron Fuller, was that the aircraft flew in formation,

Baltimore Mk11 aircraft of No 55 Squadron on their way to a
target to the West of El Alamein
Photo:RAF Museum P014682

Shadows created by a box formation of 6 Baltimores from
No 55 Squadron
Photo: Ron Fuller

usually three boxes of six aircraft escorted by fighters, mainly Kittyhawks from No 233 Fighter Wing.The aircraft stayed in close formation until the actual bombing run when they spread out to form a broad front with about 30 metres between aircraft.The leader dropped his bombs at one second intervals and the second wave started bombing as the leader's last bomb was released.This resulted in a form of pattern bombing with about 150 bombs covering an area of 1200 by 500 metres. The bombs were usually set to explode just before contact with the ground, each sending lethal fragments over a 30 metre radius. In the Baltimore the Navigator acted as the Bomb Aimer, and a notable feature of the pre flight briefing for close support attacks was the marking of the "bomb line",-a safety line to protect our own troops. With a somewhat featureless desert this was easy enough to mark on the map but not so easy to identify from the air, especially with the distractions of Flak and natural turbulence which could be quite severe in the late morning and afternoon. There was little or no Air Traffic Control at these desert landing grounds, and engines were mostly started on a signal from the leader, with perhaps a green Very light signalling take off. The condition of the landing ground determined the pattern of take off, if the sand was very loose the aircraft were lined up six at a time, heading about 20/30 degrees off the wind with the leader on one side of the formation and the others staggered to windward, so that when taking off the wind would blow the dust to one side leaving the following aircraft in clear air.When conditions were better they took off in succession, the whole process taking about four to five minutes to get the squadron airborne and into formation. According to a German POW attacks by the Baltimores and Bostons were greatly feared, and they were nicknamed "The Imperturbables" and, in a letter to Wg Cdr Gill, John remarked that the Baltimores were better than Blenheims for "bashing the Hun".Designed as an attack bomber the Baltimore, or A30 as the Americans called it, was heavily armed, with no less than 12 Colt .300 in machine guns. The later Mark III versions replaced the two

Taking off from a desert landing ground. Although the aircraft are
Bostons and not Baltimores the photo illustrates the method
adopted by No 55 Squadron when the sand was loose.
Photo: L.L-J Collection

guns in the open mid upper gun position with a Bolton Paul turret fitted with four Browning .303 in guns, giving a total of 14 guns.

Although the Luftwaffe was, by that time, short of fighters for the defence of Rommel's columns of MT, concentrations of tanks and airfields, the Flak was often described as heavy by the returning aircrews, and there were a few losses due to enemy fire during John's time with the squadron. One of the worst days was on the 6th October, during a raid on El Dabar, which was carried out from Landing Ground 86. Flt Lt Ward in AG 811 was hit by flak and crash landed 17 miles behind enemy lines killing all on board.Another Baltimore AG 807 piloted by Sgt Hannah was hit and the crew baled out, but the air gunner Sgt Coombes was killed. A third (AG 769) was also hit, and the pilot, Plt Offr Evans, ordered the crew to bale out while he made a crash landing some 1000 metres in front of the German lines. The incident was seen by a troop of South Africans in armoured cars who raced across the desert to rescue him.

John was always leading and encouraging his crews, and was only hard on those that did not try,rewarding those that did particularly well.On the 10th of August the records show that he recommended Tony Plinston and Warrant Officer Tozer for the DFC and Flt Sgt Frost for the DFM. Nor did he forget his ground crews, putting forward several names for the award of Mention In Despatches for their hard work in keeping the aircraft flying under difficult conditions.

The bombing was not all one way,on the 31st of August LG 98, which was being used by the squadron at the time,was attacked by a formation of German bombers, Flt Sgt Payne's Baltimore, AG 794, was set on fire. The aircraft was at its dispersal site having been fuelled and bombed up ready for the next days operations, as the fire took hold the bombs exploded completely destroying the aircraft. Fortunately no one was hurt in this attack as they had wisely taken to their slit trenches.

Thought to be "B" Flight crews in front of the Squadron Ops Tent. The caravan was the C.O`s mobile office. John is possibly six from the left and standing with flying helmet.

Photo.Tony Plinston

Baltimore III with Bolton Paul Turret
Photo: Ron Fuller

As in most squadrons during the war, some aircraft and crews were lost due to flying accidents, some of which should not have occurred. On the 22nd of July 1942 Plt Offr Russell in Baltimore AG 824 misjudged a low level pass near the landing ground, hit the ground and exploded, leaving an 800 yards trail of burning wreckage and killing all on board. The squadron also had its share of "friendly fire" from British AA batteries, which sometimes assumed that any aircraft coming in from the West were German or Italian. This was particularly true at the time when the squadron was based just behind the defensive line at Alamein, which the Germans were often attacking or photographing. Many crews wore "tin hats" whilst over the target as protection against shell splinters, one or two managed to get hold of old German steel hats which fitted better over flying helmets.

Life in the desert was hard and tiring. Contrary to popular opinion summer nights in the desert can be cool, and in the winter I myself have experienced such cold that several blankets and a greatcoat were needed to keep warm. Dress regulations tended to become ignored, with desert boots or "brothel creepers" as they became known, being widely adopted along with various home made pullovers or rough and uncured sheep skin jackets. John, in keeping with most senior officers, ignored these irregularities, concentrating more on the business of training and reducing casualties to a minimum. Desert storms or the "Khamsin" as it was known, left everything covered with a fine yellow dust, penetrating into machinery and even bed rolls. Food consisted mostly of "bully beef", hard tack biscuits and tinned stew- again sand was a problem,- "char" (tea) was often brewed in a cut down biscuit tin heated by petrol poured into another tin half full of sand, to take the taste of the petrol away a match stick was placed in the water .With a permanent water shortage,-the ration was two pints per day per man for washing -, keeping clean became an art, but John was always on the lookout for ways of improving their lot. In August 1942 he negotiated with the Air Headquarters Egypt for his

70

squadron to use the Transit Camp at Aboukir, near Alexandria, for their leave periods, where they could relax and above all have a fresh water shower and sleep in a sand free bed. Also in August John persuaded the staff of No 3 South African Wing to hold an athletics meeting, and on the 17th he arranged for the band of the Imperial Light Horse to give a concert for the squadron. John was also aware that morale became low if the troops were not fully occupied. During the September stand down all the air gunners were given training in rifle drill, bayonet practise and footdrill-no doubt as a result of John`s painful experiences in Sumatra and Java.

The efforts of 55 Squadron under John` command were recognised by Air Marshal Tedder, who paid a visit on the 5th September to congratulate them on a very fine performance in helping to keep the Africa Corps at bay during the critical weeks before the British offensive at Alamein. During the battle the eight Baltimore and Mitchell squadrons flew 1,200 sorties, of which 55 Squadron flew over 350.

Although on paper John had been posted to the Headquarters MEAF with effect from the 20th October, he continued to lead the squadron on operations during the battle of Alamein, and did not physically leave the squadron until the 8th of November 1942, four days after flying his last operational sortie with them.By then,because the enemy was rapidly retreating out of range of the Baltimores, the squadron`s involvement was getting less and less and it was stood down for further training. He handed over to Sqn Ldr Roulston and the Squadron went on to fly operations in support of the Tunisian campaign, the landings in Sicily and the Italian campaign of 1943/44.

At the Headquarters MEAF, where, on paper, he was a controller, there was little for him to do because, as he put it in a letter to Wg Cdr Gill, the HQ did not control anything !, and he soon got himself back to flying, this time with a series of postings to Middle East Ferry Control units. These units were not, as one might imagine, ferrying aircraft about but rather carrying people and supplies, using B24 Liberators , Loadstars and Hudson aircraft. His first appointment was as OC No 6 Ferry Control Unit at Landing Ground 224 (Cairo West) in January 1943, and the records show that he signed the unit 540 (Op Record Book) until the April. It seems almost certain therefore that he would have met Mr Churchill and other VIPs who were being flown around the Middle East in the February. He was next posted, on paper again, to Number 1 Ferry Control Unit , also located at LG 224, but there are no direct references to him by name in the units records, which appears to have been under the command of a Wg Cdr Flemming at the time, except for a note that instructions had been received on the 6th May, posting him to Number 3 Ferry Unit at Sheik Ottman near Aden. Number 3 Ferry Units records show that he was posted in, on paper again, as OC on the 6th May, and to take over from Wg Cdr Streatfield, but on the 15th May a Sqn Ldr King assumed temporary command. Later, in No 3 Ferry Units records, there is reference to an instruction, received on the 27th May for John's posting to HQ RAF(ME) for home posting. It seems likely therefore that John spent very little time at these units, although there is a reference to a 216 Group Meeting on the 1st March 1943 to which John went as OC 6 Ferry Unit. It is therefore rather difficult to determine exactly what John was doing during this period, but it seems that he probably got his hands on several different types of heavy aircraft in preparation for his posting to Bomber Command in the UK.

Notes:

1. In July 1942 the 12th Bombardment Group of the USAMEAF under the command of Colonel Charles Goodrich arrived in the Canal Zone of Egypt, having flown without loss from Florida via the Accension Islands. 81 and 82 Squadrons were initially based at Devesoir, and 83 at Ismailia, but like 55 Sqn they often operated from other landing grounds closer to the front.The American Group operated under the control of No 3 SAAF and No 232 Wing RAF. The earlier arrival of the Baltimore and Boston aircraft which were being used by the British was a result of the Lease /Lend agreement.

L.L.-J

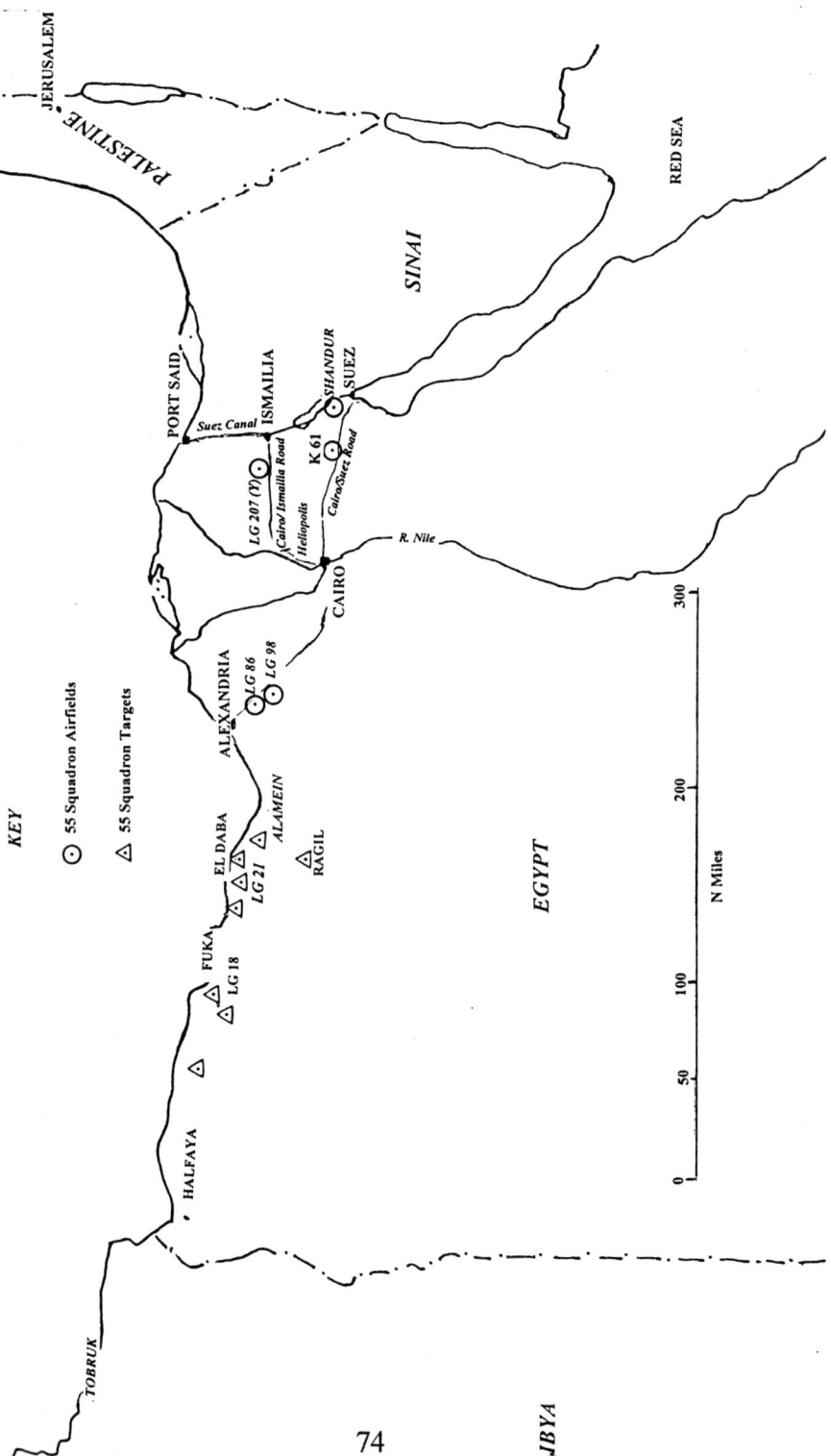

55 SQUADRON LOCATIONS AND TARGETS
JULY - NOVEMBER 1942

KEY

⊙ 55 Squadron Airfields

△ 55 Squadron Targets

JERUSALEM

PALESTINE

RED SEA

SINAI

PORT SAID

ISMAILIA

SHANDUR

SUEZ

Suez Canal

K 61

LG 207 (?)

Cairo/Ismailia Road

Cairo-Suez Road

Heliopolis

R. Nile

CAIRO

ALEXANDRIA

LG 86

LG 98

EL DABA

ALAMEIN

FUKA

LG 21

LG 18

RAGIL

EGYPT

HALFAYA

TOBRUK

LIBYA

0   50   100   200   300

N Miles

Summary of Operations Carried Out by Wg/Cdr J R. Jeudwine in No 55 Squadron July to November 1942

Date/Time	Aircraft	Crew	Base	Target	Remarks
July 25 ?	AG 814	P/O Hornby F/Sgt Perkins P/O Skillicorn	LG 98	En MT Deu Abayd	With 6 other a/c of 223 Sqn Bombed from 7000' 250lb bombs
Aug 4 0959-1120	AG 814	As above	LG "Y"	En MT GR 873285	As above plus Photos taken
Aug 9 0608-0802	AG 830	As above*	LG "Y"	LG 104 El Daba	During the period 9-16 Aug six crews were detached to 3 SA Wing to help ferry a/c to Malta
Aug 14 0606-0750	As above	As above	LG "Y"	MT North of LG 18	
Aug 16 1417-1545	As above	As above	LG 98	Tanks and MT	
Aug 25 1127-1248	AG 834	As above	LG 98	Tanks and MT	500lb bombs used Heavy AA fire

75

Date/Time	Aircraft		Base	Target	Notes
Sep 1 0707-0827	AG 767C	As above	LG 86	Tanks Deir el Ragil	Full Sqn plus fighter escort from 233 Wing Heavy AA fire..One a/c badly hit.Landed LG86 Nine others holed.
Sep 2 1413-1527	AG 824 H	As above	LG 86	Concentration of Vehs Deir el Ragil	6 a/c from 55 Sqn plus 9 Bostons from 12 Sqn SAAF .
Sep 3 0937-1100	AG 767C	As above	LG 86	Deir el Ragil	Third raid of the day

* The name McBeath appears in place of Perkins

There was a break in operations until the end of September while the Sqn moved to Kilo 61 for refresher training on Baltimore 111s.Control of Sqn passed from 3 SA Wing to 232 Wing RAF

Oct 6   See narrative. Three aircraft lost

Date/Time	Aircraft		Base	Target	Notes
Oct 9 0917-1100	AG 767	As above	LG 86	El Dabar	Raid 1
1547-1745	AG 767	As above	LG 86	LG 104	Raid 2
Oct 21 1144-1323	?	As above	LG 86	LG 21	

Date/Time		Aircraft		Base	Target	Remarks
Oct 24 0916-1038	?	AH 144C	As above ?	LG 86	Close support Battle of Alamein	Assisted by USAAFME
Oct 25 0726-0837	AH 144C		As above ?	LG 86	Close support	Watched tank battle from air
Oct 26 ?	AH 144C		As above?	LG 86	Close support	12 a/c from 55 plus 6 B25 from 82 Sqn
Oct 27 0810-1000	AH 144C		?	LG 86	LG 18	Full Sqn plus 233 Wing
1440-1600	?		?	LG 86	Tanks.Aqqaquir	6 a/c from 55 plus 6 B25 from 83 Sqn USAAFME.Raid 4
Oct 28 1349-1500	?		?	LG86	1,000 MT plus 100 tanks Aqqaquir	
Oct 29 1344-1455	?		?	LG86	Tanks and MT Aqqaquir	Two a/c badly holed All returned
Oct 30 1612-1726	AH 144C		?	LG 86	MT and AFVs Bir Sultan Omar	Six en a/c seen but no combats
Nov 2 1100-1245	AH 144C		?	LG 86	MT	One a/c holed but all all returned

77

Date/Time				Target	Notes
Nov 3 0811-0901	AH 144C	Original?	LG 86	MT	Twelve from 55 plus 6 B25 from 82 Sqn USAAFME. Five a/c badly holed but returned
1247-1424	AH 144C	?	LG 86	MT on coast road near Fuka/Al Daba	Raid 3
1523-1720	AH 144C	Original?	LG 86	As above	Raid 5
Nov 4 1230-1357	AH 144C	Original?	LG 86	MT	Raid .21 a/c from 55 Sqn plus fighter escort. Last op with 55 Sqn

Due to the swift retreat of the enemy No 55 Squadron's involvement in the battle became limited and more training was carried during November.

Chapter 4

Bomber Command

Wing Commander John Jeudwine disembarked in England on the **12th of August 1943** after three and a half years of continuous service overseas. After all the excitement of the Far East and his two periods in Egypt he took only seven days leave. It is possible that he was offered more, but he disliked sitting around at home whilst the war was going on around him. He was however pleased to get away from the dust and heat of Egypt, and to be able to walk once again through the green countryside and enjoy a pint or two of English beer, however weak or warm, at his local pub. Much of his short leave was spent reflecting on the happenings of the past three years, in particular the horrific events in Java and, most of all, the terrible decisions he had to make as regards who he should take in the "Scorpion"; the look on the faces of Dave Russel and Geoff Palmer as he left them on the beach at Tjilatjap would haunt him forever. He had covered thousands of miles by air and sea, had lost all the aircraft and nearly all the men of his first command and endured extreme physical hardship. Yet in spite of all this he had returned to the war as soon as possible and had become a very successful commander of No 55 Medium Bomber Squadron, playing an important part in the British offensive at Alamein, during which he took part in more than 25 operational missions against a determined enemy. In the last two years he had gained more experience of command and air operations than most men picked up during the whole six years of war.

Whilst at home with his mother and grandmother he visited his father's grave near Eascote in Middlesex. A sad occasion for he had seen little of his family during his early years. Boarding school, Cranwell and his pre-war service in HMS "Glorious" had robbed him of the many memories that most families have of their early years. He also took a little time to view the damage done by the Luftwaffe during the Blitz on London, and this made him determined to get into Bomber Command and to try and redress the balance as soon as possible. However before he could do this he had to learn to fly in all weathers and at night, to master the new four engined bombers which had come into service and to practise avoiding well directed enemy searchlights, anti aircraft fire and night fighters.

The first part of his training involved a two week course at No 1501 Beam Approach Training Flight near Stanton Harcourt in Oxfordshire. He joined the course on the 12th September 1943, along with two other Wing Commanders, Jefferson and Baird-Smith, and a Squadron Leader Powell. Here he flew Oxford trainers and learned to make approaches to airfields in bad weather. Later, in September, he moved to No 28 Operational Training Unit (OTU) at Wymeswold in Leicestershire. Here he selected some of the aircrew with whom he was to fly with on future operations. Selecting the right crew at OTUs was very important because the integrity and mutual confidence of the crew members could mean their survival when it came to dealing with difficult situations in the air. John looked around for the more experienced and older men, for rear gunner he chose "Johnny" Johnson-Biggs, who had been in the RAF since 1935. As both had already had a considerable amount of combat experience they were able to pass on a lot of good advice to the younger members .

Their time at Wymeswold seems to have formed the basis for a very happy and successful crew. Their trips together to the local pubs lead to some amusing escapades, Johnson-Biggs recalls- "One night we were short of transport so the skipper carried me all the way on the crossbar of his bike, being taller than

I was he was just about able to see where he was going, but there were several near misses and a lot of laughter."

The more serious side of the training, flying in Wellington twin engined bombers, involved learning how to dodge enemy night fighters by "corkscrewing" and diving when coned in searchlights. Practise raids, dropping leaflets, known as "Nickel" operations, were made over France. These raids often acted as diversions for the main bomber force by confusing the German fighter controllers.

In November the crew moved on to 1668[1] Heavy Conversion Unit (HCU) at Balderton. Here they met up with the remaining members of the seven man crew required for the four engined Lancaster bombers. Some members of the crew had been together before but had been returned to base from operational squadrons because their pilots had been lost whilst flying as second pilots on their first operation.[2] Most of the new pilots at the HCU were wary of taking on such crews, believing there was a "jinx" on them, but John again chose the more experienced, preferring them to the "kids straight out of school." John's first selected crew consisted of -
the navigator, Flt Sgt Leonard Eric Gosling from Coventry; the bomb aimer, Sgt Edwin Booth a married man from Leeds; the flight engineer, Sgt Charles Fryer (known as "Tuck") who had been an apprentice at RAF Halton; the radio operator, Sgt Alec Shaw Bates from Cheshire; mid upper gunner, Flt Sgt Leslie Birch a big Australian; and the tail gunner, Flg Offr W. Johnson- Biggs who has already been mentioned.

The degree of comradeship in the crew can be judged by a small incident related by Alec Bates;- "When we first met the skipper at 1668 HCU we noticed that his battledress blouse was a little untidy, notably his OBE ribbon was hanging on by a thread. Teddy produced a needle and thread and sewed it on again. As soon as John went to put the blouse on again he noticed what had been done. For a while he said nothing, then gave way to his

81

favourite form of mock admonishment- *I am not going to ask who did this because I know you will all keep quiet, but I reckon you are a gang of witch doctors and I have half a mind to post you all to Karachi !"*

John and this crew flew some 30 hours at the HCU, 15 by day and 15 by night, rather less than usual due to John's previous experience. Summing up John's time at the HCU the chief instructor, Sqn Ldr Gunter recalls,- "I knew he was a very experienced pilot, but I never had the opportunity to discuss his previous exploits. It was typical of the man that in modesty he did not talk about them, I had the impression that he was very keen to have a go at the enemy in Europe"

On the 1st December 1943 John was posted as Commanding Officer of No 619 Squadron based, at that time, at Woodhall Spa in Lincolnshire.

John arrived at No 619 Squadron on the **2nd of December 1943,** just after the start of the Battle of Berlin. Air Marshal Harris had decided to use all the forces under his command to destroy Berlin, the centre of Nazism and the capital of the Third Reich. He aimed to bring the Germans to their knees by sending bombers night after night to destroy their main towns and cities. For four months waves of Lancasters and Halifax bombers dropped tons of bombs on to the capital and sixteen other large towns and cities including Leipzig, Frankfurt, Stuttgart, Brunswick, Magdeburg and Ausburg.

This was one of the most difficult periods for Bomber Command. Weather conditions were not good and the enemy defended their homeland with great vigour, their guns and night fighters creating unbelievable damage to the bomber streams. The chances of a bomber crew surviving a tour of 30 operations grew less and less. The men had to contend with intense cold-often 30°C below zero- aircraft iced up and on return to the UK the crews, tired after a seven or eight hour flight, were often confronted with low cloud or fog over their home base, forcing them to land at another base or bale out and leave the aircraft to crash into the sea. It was into this situation that John arrived at Woodhall Spa to take command of his first heavy bomber squadron.The Base Commander and friend, Air Commodore Sharp, introduced John to his predecessor Wing Commander Abercromby, and in company with Station Commanders, Group Captains Patch and Evans-Evans, he visited his future squadron to watch the crews take off to Berlin, and later to attend the debriefing. Two crews from 619 Squadron were missing, those of Plt Offr Ward and Fg Offr Bower. Wg Cdr Abercromby had lead the squadron and had been accompanied by an American War Correspondent, Ed Murrow, who later published an article describing the raid which gained him the Pulitzer Prize.Two other journalists went on the raid, Capt Grieg of the Daily Mail and Norman Stocton of the Sydney Sun, neither returned having perished with two Australian crews of No 460 Squadron. Altogether that night the Luftwaffe night fighters had added another 40 aircraft to their mounting score of four- engined bombers.

On the morning of the 3rd December fog again covered the Lincolnshire countryside and there was no flying. The ground crews however were kept busy preparing for the next operation planned for the following night, but in spite of their efforts only seven aircraft could be made ready in time.The target was Leipzig and John flew in Lancaster "P" as "Second Dicky" to Sqn Ldr Aytoun, a very experienced pilot. At the usual briefing, the Station Commander informed the crews of the change of command, wished Abercromby good luck in his new appointment and introduced John as the new Commanding Officer.

The seven Lancasters took off just after midnight. The bombing was apparently successful but casualties were again high; 24 aircraft missing or 4.6% of the total force. This was John's first operation in a Lancaster and in the skies of North West Europe; a very different scene from the Far East or North Africa. I wonder

Lancasters of No 619 Squadron. The Squadron Code is PG, the leading aircraft S. Jeudwine's favourite aircraft, "Nulli Secundus" was coded PG-A. *Original photo IWM*

what went through his mind as he encountered for the first time the formidable anti- aircraft defences, the radar controlled searchlights and guns, nightfighters and all the flares and other pyrotechnics dropped by the Pathfinders ?

On the 4th December John officially took command, Wing Commander Abercromby was posted as OC No 83 (PFF) Squadron and it is sad to relate that he was killed during a raid on Berlin less than a month later. John immediately set about getting to know his men and trying to improve their morale which had suffered during the recent heavy losses. Always encouraging, he was helped in this process by a "stand down" for about two weeks when the weather was particularly bad and prevented any operations.The time was spent in ground training such as practice for "ditching", and in sport such as football and cross country running, which was of course John's first love.

On the 16th December the weather cleared; the base shook off its lethargy and "Ops" were on again. The target was again Berlin. No 619 Sqn put up fifteen aircraft and one was lost. Another 24 aircraft from the main force were missing but worse still 29 aircraft crashed or were abandoned due to dense fog and low cloud once again covering the home airfields. On the 20th December John led the full squadron for the first time with his own crew, the target was Frankfurt. Their Lancaster that night was code letter "N" serial number LM 419 which had been built at the Avro factory Leadon near Leeds in 1943, unfortunately the aircraft was lost in the hands of another crew during a raid on Schweinfurt in the following February. Of the fifteen squadron aircraft that went to Frankfurt, one, piloted by Fg Offr Thompson, returned early with an engine on fire and two were missing. Twelve aircraft bombed successfully dropping 56 tons of bombs. Losses amongst the main force amounted to 41 aircraft - 6.3%.

On the 23rd December crews were briefed for another operation, but as night fell so did the temperature and the aircraft became covered with ice which could not be cleared. The operation was cancelled and the crews crawled gratefully into their beds. The following morning the aircraft were disarmed and the bombs taken back to the dump-a difficult task in the freezing weather. Being Christmas eve the messes were decorated and on Christmas Day, according to tradition, the officers and Senior NCOs served dinner in the airmen's mess and a concert was arranged with Mrs Hemingway in attendance.

Operations were again cancelled on the Boxing Day, which was just as well after a rather heavy night in the messes, instead everyone was "invited" to take part in a cross country run-just the thing John advised for getting the brain back into working order !.

The next operation took place on the 29th December, Berlin again, with John leading. Fifteen aircraft were made ready but one, Plt Offr Taylor, did not take off due to some technical fault. All the squadron returned safely and losses overall were lighter-only 2.8%
. A mission was planned for New Year's Day but was cancelled much to the relief of the crews who were then able to celebrate the new year in the normal manner. On New Year's Day, after a rather painful reveille, the aircraft were prepared for yet another trip to Berlin. Fourteen aircraft were sent from 619 Squadron but one returned early with three engines giving trouble. John did not go on this raid but all the crews got home safely. The raid was not a success due to the target being cloud covered, and the losses were again high with 6.7% of the total force missing. Next night it was Berlin again and this time John led nine other Lancasters from the squadron, one, Flt Lt McGilroy in "O" returned early with problems and two others, "H" flown by Flt Lt Cox and "D" by Fg Offr Hefferman did not return, adding to the 25 other Lancasters out of a total of 362 , a loss of 7% .It seems that the German controllers had accurately predicted the target and the night fighters were waiting for the bombers over the target area.

On the **5th January** the target changed to Stettin, not bombed since 1941. A force of 358 aircraft, including 12 from John's squadron, put in a successful attack although sadly Fg Offr

Day in "A" serial ED977 [3] failed to return, his was the oldest aircraft in the squadron having been built at Avro's Manchester factory in 1942. On the 28th January John took over a new aircraft, Serial No LL 778, which had only recently rolled off the production line at an Armstrong Whitworth factory. It was given the Squadron code letter "A" and he named it "Nulli Secundus"-Second to None- It was during his first trip in this aeroplane that he had a major problem whilst returning from Berlin. Alec Bates recalls the incident;- " We were on our way back from Berlin when the rear gunner began behaving very strangely, singing rude songs and not answering when called on the intercom. He was obviously suffering from hypoxia. The skipper called me and asked me to go and see what was happening. I picked up my portable oxygen bottle and went back to the rear turret. The turret was stationary and on the quarter. I opened the rear doors and thumped Johnson-Biggs on the back with no effect. I then tried to pull him out of the turret but only succeeded in rocking him backwards and forwards.I glanced at the guage on my oxygen bottle -to my horror I saw it was nearly empty. Back I went to my radio, and the skipper called "Tuck" to try. In a few minutes "Tuck" came blundering back vomitting and bleeding from the nose. He climbed **over** the navigator instead of moving behind him. Then there were gurgling noises from the navigator, in climbing over him "Tuck" had disconnected his oxygen supply. I needed no further instruction, I reached round and reconnected Goslings mask, slapped his face and he came to life. Another call from the skipper, this time to tell Les the mid upper gunner, to try and get the rear gunner out, and for me to take over the mid upper turret. Eventually Les managed to get "Johnny" out of his turret and get some oxygen into him. On the return of Les I went back to my radio. Quite enough excitement for one night you might say, but while I had been away from the radio I had missed important wind changes broadcast by Bomber Command, and as a result we became separated from the main bomber stream and wandered into the flak belts along the Baltic coast. All this with only one turret working. We were lucky to survive, even the skipper, normally so cool and collected remarked afterwards *-when the navigator passed out I nearly gave up !* " Johnson -Biggs survived but with bad frostbite. He was hospitalised and did not fly again with that crew. His own version of events are understandably a little at variance, but his account follows. -

"The target was Berlin on the 28/29th January 1944. Time over target 0240hrs, height 22,000 feet.It was one of the coldest nights I had ever experienced and I remember having to scrape the ice off the perspex before take off. Over the target I noticed two aircraft go down in flames, I informed the skipper and stated that the flak and searchlights were intense. At that time I seemed to have trouble with my oxygen supply, I was feeling sick and terribly cold. I tried to increase my oxygen supply without succes and it seems that I eventually passed out. The skipper sent the flight engineer to help me, and he managed to get me out of the turret and put another mask on my face but it seems that I pulled that one off too. Anyway in all the confusion we got off course and separated from the main stream-not a happy situation. Eventually we made it back to base, thanks to our pilot who was an excellent skipper. On return to base I was taken to sick quarters and then transferred to the RAF hospital at Rauceby. During my time in hospital I was visited by the Wing Commander and other members of the crew, -they could hardly recognize me with my face all swollen with frost bite.After a month I was sent on two months sick leave before being passed fit for flying, but I never flew with the Wing Commander again. Later, after two trips with Plt Offr Powell in my place, he managed to get the Base gunnery leader, Flt Lt Jack Howard, a very experienced rear gunner, as a permanent replacement."

Bad weather in the first two weeks of February provided another breathing space for Bomber Command and John once again seized upon the opportunity to carry out more training. The

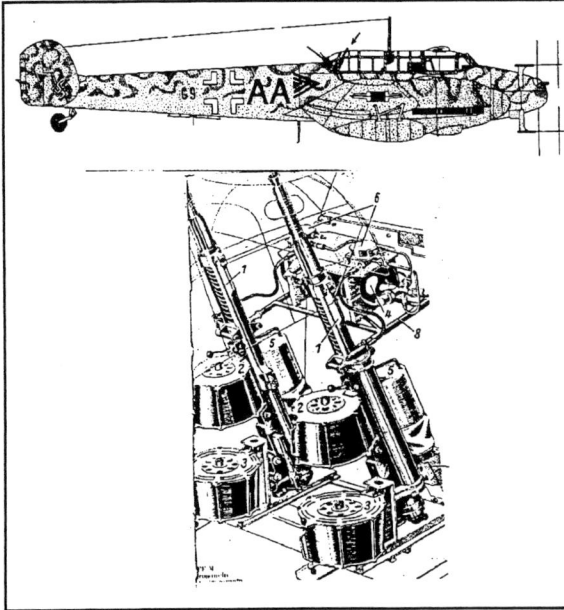

"Schrage Musik".The two upward and forward firing cannon in the Me 110. The night fighter pilot would position his aircraft under the bombers -in the blind spot- match the speeds and open fire.

Flt Lt Jack Howard DFC, Jeudwine's rear gunner in the Lancaster

next operation was on the 15th February and was the largest force ever sent to Berlin. Harris sent nearly 900 heavy bombers of which 20 came from John's squadron including one borrowed from 630 Squadron. There was one early return from 619 Squadron and Fg Offr Rumble and his crew failed to return- the first squadron loss in February.

On the 19th February the squadron provided 19 aircraft for a raid against Leipzig but John was not with them. In spite of appalling casualties amongst the main force -9.5% all the squadron aircraft returned safely. Most of the losses were the result of enemy night fighters getting into the bomber stream- the loss amounted to the equivalent of four complete squadrons. On the 20th February John led the squadron to Stuttgart, which was bombed from a height of 21,000 ft, but the bombing was rather scattered due once again to cloud cover. One squadron aircraft flown by Sqn Ldr Fuller was damaged near the target by debris from a Lancaster which exploded close by. John's eighth operation with Bomber Command took place on the 24th February against the important ball bearing plant at Schweinfurt.The Americans had already made a daylight raid and the night raid was judged a great success, as recorded earlier it was here that Fg Offr Williams was lost flying in "N" -John's old aircraft.

February ended with an attack on Augsburg. Fifteen of the squadron went off, but John had to stay behind due to an imminent visit by the Secretary of State for Air. Happily all the crews returned and the raid was successful. The Station then had a stand down until the end of the month.

During March 1944 plans were being drawn up for a new phase of the air war. Air Marshal Harris was under pressure to abandon his attacks on Berlin and to concentrate instead on targets in France and Belgium in preparation for the forthcoming invasion of Normandy by Allied troops. The new targets were the enemy's aircraft factories, railway repair shops, rail yards and ammunition dumps.The attacks were to be made at low level in order to minimise casualties amongst the French civilians.Crews were taking extra risks by coming down to the ceiling of the lighter anti-aircraft guns, and had clear orders to bring their bombs home if they could not positively identify the aiming points. The forces sent on these raids were generally smaller, being typically 100 or 200 aircraft, and the attacks were made with the help of new techniques of target marking and the use of a controller who became known as the Master Bomber.

There were however several important raids on Germany by Bomber Command Squadrons in March 1944. The first was to Stuttgart with John leading 15 aircraft, and this was the first time he took Jack Howard as his rear gunner. Jack was a very experienced man, and probably knew more about deflection shots from the tail end of a Lancaster than most, and he willingly became a member of the crew on future operations. All the squadron aircraft returned safely from this operation.

John's first operation over France was on the 10th March when ten Lancasters from the squadron were part of a small force which attacked an aircraft factory at Chateauroux in central France. Being the first of this type of operation the Base Commander, Air Commodore A.C.H. Sharp, flew with John as an observer. The attack was judged as a complete success, and described by the crews in the vernacular of the day as "a piece of cake".

On the **24th March** Bomber Command turned their attention once again to Berlin. John led 17 aircraft from 619 Squadron which was part of a force of over 800 aircraft that took off for "The Big City". The weather was dreadful, the night becoming known as "The night of the strong winds", which set the main stream well to the South of the target area. But the weather was also bad for the Luftwaffe, and it was Flak that accounted for most of the 72 aircraft that never saw their dispersal areas again. Plt Offr Thompson and his crew were lost, it was only their second operation, and John had the sad task of writing the seven letters informing the relatives that the aircraft was missing.

In April, with "Overlord" only two months away, England became an immense military dump, a sort of giant aircraft carrier. Everywhere in the country camps grew like mushrooms and Americans, Canadians, French, Norwegian and Poles were to be seen in ever increasing numbers. The number of airfields was also increasing, so much so that it was joked that you could get from one to another just by taxying ! Life for the civilian population became increasingly difficult as first one then another area was subjected to restrictions, this was particularly true in the South of the country where the troops were concentrating for the forthcoming D Day landings. Pubs were full of GIs and many of the old British customs began to change.At one time three million men were gathered together for the forthcoming landings in France. All day and at night there were incessant comings and goings of lorries, tanks and troop trains, and the sound of aircraft broke the quiet of the English countryside, some joked that the Island would sink under the weight of arms and men that arrived every day.

April also brought the first signs of better weather, with flowers and trees bursting into life. Looking around them the soldiers and civilians guessed that all this amount of men and materials could only mean one thing- that the invasion was imminent and that there was soon to be a third front in Europe, which after those of Italy and Russia might prove too much for the German army; how could they possibly fight on three fronts at once ?. Hope for an early end to the war, the end of the slaughter, the deprivation and a return to peace became the motivation for all the men and women engaged in the common fight against the Nazi tyranny. Nearly every one had a brother, son, daughter, husband or father who was fighting somewhere,and everyone wanted to end it once and for all and to take part in the final push to bring about Hitler's defeat.

But the winter also ended in a tragedy for Bomber Command. This was the raid on Nurenburg on the 30th March, no less than 95 bombers were lost out of a force of less than 800

-nearly 12%. The losses were so great that it took several days to re-equip and re-inforce the squadrons with aircraft and crews and it was as well that the weather prevented operations during the first few days of April. John took advantage of the situation and set about more training for his crews, with navigation exercises and dinghy drill.

5th April. Operation Toulouse.The target was an aircraft factory, and the raid marked the start of a new low level marking technique using a Mosquito. The new system of marking was devised by Wg Cdr Leonard Cheshire, "Micky" Martin of 617 Sqn and the staff of the newly formed 5 Group Marking Force which had been set up at 54 Base. Cheshire flew in fast and low and on the third pass dropped his markers right on target. The two earlier runs had given the French factory workers time to take cover. The training for this new type of marking and control led to the installation of a very complex training device which was built at Coningsby, Alec Bates takes up the story;- "The device consisted of a revolving table with a model of the target on top. The front end of a Lancaster was perched above it and weather and lighting effects could be varied from full moon to total darkness. The slowly revolving table would give the bomb aimer and pilot the impression that they were circling the target, the whole model was exactly to scale and in my spare time I helped Molly, one of our Sergeant WAAF watchkeepers, to paint in the fields."

John led 13 of his squadron aircraft on the raid again accompanied by A/Cdre Sharp. Being a rather dominant character Sharp tended to take charge of events, and on the way home, having received diversion instructions, insisted on landing at Westcott which was near his home rather than at Carnaby which had been ordered. However the raid was a great success, and Air Marshal Harris was so impressed by the results that he informed AVM Cochrane that 5 Group could go ahead with arrangements to form its own marking force, and that he would transfer two Lancaster squadrons- 83 and 97 from 8 (PFF) Group and 627 Sqn

Mosquitoes -to No 5 Group for the purpose. This was a blow for AVM Bennett, AOC of No 8(PFF) Group,who claimed that he had never been properly consulted on the matter, and some bitter arguments took place. Group Captain "Benny" Goodman, who was a pilot on No 627 Sqn at the time, describes the change-. "One day after our move to Woodhall Spa we were conveyed by bus to Coningsby where we were directed to the station cinema. Here were assembled all the crews of 83 and 97 Lancaster Pathfinder Squadrons, our own squadron and the AOC and his entourage including Leonard Cheshire. The AOC opened the meeting by saying that a number of successful attacks had been made by 617 Sqn on important pinpoint targets and it was now intended to repeat these on a wider scale. The Lancaster Pathfinder squadrons were to identify the target on H2S and were to lay a carpet of flares, under which 627 Sqn would locate and mark the precise aiming points for the main force to bomb. So that was it-we were to become low level markers and it all sounded rather dangerous ! "

Cheshire was the next to speak, and he explained carefully how the low level marking was done, the Lancasters had to lay a carpet of hooded flares, the light from which would be directed downwards onto the target without blinding the bomb aimers. A small force of Mosquitoes-four or possibly six- would orbit, identify the aiming point and then mark it in a shallow dive with 500lb red spot fires.The Marker Leader would then assess the positions of the markers in relation to the aiming point and pass the information on to the Master of Ceremonies or Master Bomber as he was to become, who would be flying in one of the Lancasters .The Master Bomber would then take over and direct the main force aircraft in their attack.

John Jeudwine was in fact among the AOC`s "entourage" at this meeting, and he became very interested in the description of the new technique and by the accuracy of the bombing that had been achieved; ever since his days dive bombing in Hawker Harts he had always considered precision bombing to be better, and this new system seemed to have the best of both worlds, accuracy and yet the ability to deliver a great weight of bombs, he decided that "this was for him" and he requested a transfer to 54 Base as a Master Bomber.

John knew the dangers of becoming a Master Bomber, flying around in the target area he would become easy prey for German night fighters who were attracted by the flares like moths to a candle. He also knew that to survive, his crew had to be better trained than most, and he therefore organised extra training in fighter affiliation and accurate bombing.

In the early raids on targets in France Bomber Command's losses were much less than they had been in attacks on the German homeland. This was partly due to the fact that the German night fighters were mostly concentrated in Holland, Belgium and Germany itself. As a result Bomber Command decided that trips to France would only count as one third of an operation towards the total of 30 for a complete tour. Later however, after heavy losses at Mailly Le Camp, the idea of "one third" of an operation was dropped.The Luftwaffe was also suffering from a lack of pilots,with units melting like ice under the sun, disappearing in the furnace of the Eastern Front, or being swallowed up in the fight with American fighters escorting the waves of Flying Fortresses and Liberators bombing Germany.

10th April. John made a test flight before lunch in preparation for his first attack as Master Bomber on the important railway junction St Pierre des Corps on the East side of Tours in the Loire Valley.The target comprised a locomotive repair shop, depot and marshalling yard. It was not an easy target for the planners because it was surrounded by the houses of railway workers and on the other side of the river there was an important German fighter airfield which was very well defended by light and medium anti aircraft batteries, with the lighter guns being mounted on towers and backed up by the formidable 88mm guns. The German base had already been bombed by the American 8th USAAF but without any great success. The base usually held 1SKG 10 which was equipped with FW 190s which were becoming increasingly used as night fighters, having taken part in the "baby blitz" of 1943.The attack took place without any great problem, John controlled the 180 Lancasters taking part with great efficiency, 1,200 high explosive bombs and a great number of incendiaries were dropped and the Eastern part of the marshalling yards was badly damaged. Only one bomber was missing. A railway worker who was on duty that night has given this account of the raid;-

" I was on duty that night from 2100hrs to 0700hrs at the station of St Pierre des Corps. At 0110hrs we had two trains to receive and to send to Nantes.A little before the first train was due to arrive some Allied aircraft released flares on small parachutes.There were several hundred and we could see very clearly. We had been warned that a serious raid might take place, because there had already been several attacks on other towns in the West. There was no question of letting a train into the station, so after the first was gone I returned to the office but there was no one there except a German railway agent who said in a terrible accent- *I believe that the raid will begin soon, no ?* I answered - I think so too, we must go to the shelter. This shelter was reached by a door in the North side of the underground way which connected the station platforms. Coming into the shelter we were joined by two *grey mice* (female auxilliaries of the German army) then by an engine driver and his stoker and finally by eight German soldiers.The phone rang, it was a colleague who asked me *-how many of you are there down there-and* says *-my poor old man, let me know when it is all over.* At the same time the first bombs fell, it was 0132hrs. We listened to the rumble of the aircraft and the whistling of the bombs. There was a slight lull in the middle of the attack but suddenly a bomb fell not far from our shelter and smoke came into the shelter through a gap in the roof. Then an even greater explosion blew in the door of the shelter right on to the Germans, they stood up grumbling *-mein gott.* I was unharmed being protected by a recess in the wall. No one spoke, even the stoker who had earlier made jokes because , being squatted down he saw the buttocks of one of the German auxiliaries !. At 0254hrs the bombing stopped and I tried to telephone but all the lines were down.We went out, the station was on fire from one end to the other, my bicycle and sandwiches were in my office which was on fire, the only other living thing seemed to be a very frightened little goat that was bleating. I went to my house and my companions scattered. The buildings in Station Street were in flames, turning night into day. Further on by the church things were not so bad but a man called out to me *be careful, there are some holes in the middle of the street!* In fact these holes, 80cm wide, turned out to be delayed action bombs.Arriving at my house I found it had not been damaged. Not having anything else to do I returned to the station to find more people than before, Station Master, Prefect, some Boche and a few friends. I was asked to stay and help clear up.. After a while there was a large explosion, then another, and another, it was the delayed action bombs. A friend arrived looking very pale- *lads there is one very close !-* we risked being flattened so we ran further away."

The delayed action bombs continued to explode for several weeks delaying the repair work on the railway and causing more damage and casualties. The official state of damage was according to French sources;-400 buildings destroyed, 300 damaged, 10 killed, 53 injured severely and 41 lightly. Unfortunately on the 17th April, seven days after the raid a team of young repair workers were caught by an unexploded bomb and another 10 were killed and 6 more injured.

The next night, the 11th April, orders were received for yet another operation, but John`s crew were due for some leave and , having made a test flight to make sure that some "Gremlins" had been removed from the aircraft, the crew scrounged lifts to Tattershall station for their train. It was their first leave since February, they were tired and needed the rest.Alec Bates the

Wireless Operator remembers- "We were supposed to get nine days leave every six weeks. If after about five weeks John showed no signs of wanting leave we used to tell him his landings were getting rougher than usual and he needed a rest. He would ask- *whatever do you do on leave?* His favourite form of chiding was to call us "witch doctors" and threaten to post us all to Karachi !" In spite of all this the crew were very loyal and united, and they worked well as a team. They all came from very different backgrounds and parts of the country, all had the greatest confidence in John`s ability to get them out of a tight spot. Most described him as a very quiet person, they never asked and he never spoke of his family. On the base he was "The Winco", but in the air he was just the skipper or John. Like most aircrews they kept together on their nights off, and John would join them for a drink at the local pubs like the *Blue Bell Inn* on the road to Woodhall or at the *Mucky Duck* at Coningsby, where they would enjoy a few hours of freedom from the constant threat of a "chop night", and recharge their reserves of courage which would keep them going towards that seemingly unobtainable goal of 30 operations and the end of their tour.

John as usual stayed on the base, and monitored the preparations for the night op to come. As night fell he watched his squadron take off for a raid on the rail yards at Aachen and with the Base Commander waited for their return. When they finally arrived back in the early hours of the 12th April two crews were missing, John asked one of the WAAFs on duty to check with other airfields to see if they had landed there. There was no news and eventually the WAAF said " they would have run out of fuel an hour ago", and sadly she wrote on the board FTR-failed to return-against the crews of Sqn Ldr McGilvray and Flt Lt Moore,-she had danced with some of them only a week ago.

While the crew was away on leave 619 Sqn was ordered to move to Dunholme Lodge, this was to make room for 83 and 97 (PFF) squadrons which had been moved over from 8 (PFF) Group as part of the setting up of the 5 Group special marking force.

Coningsby was in chaos, with movements in and out, air and ground crews piling into Lancasters with all their personal belongings and many "souvenirs" and taking off for Dunholme, while incoming crews were "bagging" the best accommodation.

Unlike Coningsby,which was a pre war airfield, Dunholme was a collection of Nissen huts spread around the village of Welton. From the airfield it was possible to see the spires of Lincoln cathedral which was only four miles away, a fact which did not pass unnoticed by the squadron airmen who reckoned it was only an hour`s walk to good pubs, girls and the cinema.

The Squadron's first operation from Dunholme was on the 18th April, when they joined 44 Squadron led by Wg Cdr F.W. Thompson for an attack on the rail yards at Juvisy. Still without his crew John spent the day making sure his squadron was fully prepared for the night's operation. As mentioned earlier John's aircraft had been named "Nulli Secundus"-second to none. He was very keen on this name, and all the squadron fitters knew that this was "The Winco`s aircraft". In fact "Nulli Secundus" was the first aircraft on the squadron with paddle propellers, and "Tuck" Fryer, the flight engineer, worked long hours with the ground crew to keep the aircraft in tip top condition. John himself was very keen to create this bond between the air and ground crews. Leslie Birch the mid upper gunner comments-

"Jeudwine was certainly a fine airman and good leader, he did not expect anyone to do what he could not do himself. In rank we were poles apart, but he always joined in on a crew party and encouraged the ground crew to come along. As a result our aircraft was always spotless and kept in good order."

The crew returned from leave on the 25th April, and John immediately took them on a test flight. On the 26th "Ops" were on again, this time to the important ball bearing plants at Schweinfurt. This was the first time a Mosquito was used for the marking, unfortunately the marking was not good and the bombing became rather scattered. German fighter opposition was intense and the squadron lost another two crews, Flt Lt Gunzi and Flt Sgt Whinfield. They were the fifth crew lost since the beginning of the month.

John's personality and qualities of leadership were appreciated throughout the whole squadron. Alec Bates again-" On the surface he was a typical Regular RAF Officer, tall, thin, sunburnt, wrinkled and older than average for a bomber skipper. He was rather aloof, perhaps shy, preoccupied and even a little sad. It was obvious that he was an above average pilot and commander. When amused he had a single hard barking laugh, just one *HA*. When given some information his favourite reply was *Oh really*, showing belief or disbelief by the intonation of the phrase. He walked around with an almost detached air and the WAAFs all thought he was wonderful. His speech was clipped, aristocratic and precise. He could be very decisive in matters of importance, but was not too proud to take advice. He and I shared something of a dislike of ceremonial parades, just occasionally we would have to attend a colour hoisting parade and Teddy, Les and I worked out a dodge for slipping out of line when the parade reached a bend in the road, slipping through a gap in the hedge and hiding in the parachute loft. John pretended to be very annoyed, but in fact he was highly amused, and apart from his favourite threat about posting us all the Karachi, he did nothing about it." Alec Bates continues- " I think he must have had a mental barrier against women, while he was always polite he had a sort of coldness towards them. There was one red haired WAAF driver who drove the crew bus. Immediately she heard that the Wing Commander had landed she would take the bus straight across the airfield, disregarding the perimeter track and regardless of any other passengers , who would be bounced about, to arrive at the aircraft before she picked up other crews, once she had him safely on board she would revert to normal sedate driving via the perimeter track to the debriefing room."Another squadron member, Reg Hutton the Engineer Leader,remembers John as a rather dour man, -

No 619 Squadron Officers 1944
Back Row: A Canadian, Engineer?, Canadian, F. Secker, R Hutton, T. Playford, K. Roberts, Aus.
Seated: Gilmour, Jeudwine.
Front: K. Graves, J. Howard, J. Dougherty.

obstinate, bold and hard. He was a better man than Cheshire or Gibson"

April had already seen a significant drop in Bomber Command's effort against targets in Germany and in May the attacks dwindled away to just three major attacks, one against Duisburg on the 21/22 May, another on the following night against Dortmund and Brunswick and the third German target, Aachen, was attacked twice at the end of the month but with comparatively few aircraft. In contrast between May and June 1944 the average number of sorties per month against German installations and the railways in France and Belgium rose to well over 12,000, compared with a monthly total in March of under 2,000. All this was of course in preparation for the Allied landings in Normandy in June.

John's first target in France during May was in the area of Toulouse. The Pink City, as it is known in France, was well known to crews of 5 Group and this time the targets were the explosive works at la Poudrerie Nationale and the aircraft assembly plant of St Martin du Touche. Because of the distance involved all aircraft had to carry some 1,800 gallons of fuel, thus limiting their bomb loads to about 11,000lbs. Twelve aircraft were detailed from 619 Squadron including those of some of "the old hands" namely Sqn Ldr Fuller, Fg Offr Secker Sqn Ldr Whamond and the Australian Flt Lt Roberts, their particular target was La Poudrerie. The twelve aircraft took off on the long trip at around 21.00hrs on the 1st of May and expected to reach the Toulouse area at about 01.35hrs the following morning. Visibility was good, with near full moon, John and Teddy Booth the bomb aimer both spotted the red target indicators at the same time whilst a few miles short of the target. These indicators were to act as a route marker and orbit area in case the marking of the aiming point should be delayed. Unfortunately the marker was not very accurately placed and as a result the flare dropping was rather scattered, however with the good visibility the target was easily identified and the Mosquitoes of 627 Squadron made their low level runs. The first aircraft, piloted by Flt Lt Steere, had a "hang up" with his marker but the second dived from 2,000 feet to release his red spot fires at 300 feet. They fell about 200 meters North East of the aiming point, but these were backed up by the controller, Sqn Ldr Simpson, who put his markers right on the target. Simpson then called in the main force to bomb, and accurate bombing took place; when smoke obscured the markers the crews were instructed to bomb on the fires which had been started. John bombed at 0140hrs from 6,700 feet. Only two enemy fighters were seen, one attacking the Lancaster of Flt Lt Houlden of 106 Squadron as he circled the target area; his mid upper gunner opened fire and the enemy was seen to break away out of sight. The flak was intense and several aircraft were hit,-mostly over the aircraft assembly plant, Sqn Ldr Mackensie of 627 Squadron had three holes in his aircraft and his friend, Fg Offr Saint-Smith, discovered a hole in the nose of his Mosquito after landing. One of the "Illuminators" of 97 Squadron , Lancaster ME 625 flown by Sqn Ldr Locke, had radio problems and he was unable to send or receive any messages over his VHF, then his port outer engine failed due to a leak of Glycol, a fire started just short of the target, but they pressed on with three engines and made their bombing run with an unserviceable rear turret. Just after the bombing run they were attacked several times by a ME 210 (perhaps the same fighter that went for Houlden) but Locke evaded skillfully and at his debrief he recorded- "Journey home accomplished on three engines without further incident !" On return to base the crew however described the night as "a shaky do", but it was a successful operation, both targets being destroyed. However there had been several problems connected with communications, marking and control and the conclusions of the final raid report make interesting reading :- "It is again stressed that the Controller should be an officer selected because of his wide service experience as well as Bomber Command experience, preferably on his second tour and not merely because he is a

Pathfinder or flare dropper. It is suggested that the flare dropping, marking and assessing the target should be left to one Controller, or Marker Leader, but from the moment that he gives the order to attack or uses a code word to signify that the marking is complete, then the Master Bomber should take charge of and direct the bombing operations, the marker squadrons being merely concerned in keeping the markers, which they themselves have assessed as satisfactory, backed up." This conclusion concerned John greatly as he was about to be selected as a controller.

John and his crew returned from the long flight to Toulouse and landed at their home base of Dunholme Lodge. Although the dangers had not been as great as a flight to "The Big City" they were very tired and, as the engines were cut, they still had the noise in their ears of the four Merlins, also, as they climbed out of the aircraft ,they found they were staggering about as if they had been drinking, the symptoms disappeared as the circulation returned to their limbs and, after debriefing, they climbed wearily into bed. John was so tired that he forwent his customary cigarette before turning in at 0630hrs.

The 3rd of May 1944. For a Spring morning it was very cold, a white frost covered the fields,-a bad day for the farmers John remarked as he left the mess. It was so cold that the ground crews wore gloves as they rode their bicycles out to the dispersal points. The day was to go down in the history books for both 1 and 5 Groups and of Bomber Command, for it was on that day that plans were made to attack the large military installation at Mailly le Camp, between Troyes and Chalons sur Marne, some 80 miles East of Paris. Mailly consisted of a large depot, repair shops and tank training area, and, at the time of the attack, units of the 21st Panzer Division were there being re-fitted and trained. The op order called for 346 heavy bombers to attack in two waves. 619 Squadron was to provide 12 Lancasters , John did not go himself, but his mid upper gunner, Leslie Birch, took part as a member of the crew of

Sqn Ldr Fuller. The raid was very successful with 102 vehicles and 37 tanks destroyed, over 200 highly trained tank crews killed and their barracks pulverized, but the losses amongst the bomber crews was unusually high for a French target. 42 aircraft out of the 346 failed to return-0ver 13%- and over 300 aircrew lost their lives. It was as bad as some of the worst nights during the winter of 1943/44 and much has been written about the causes of the disaster. Primarily it was again a matter of failed communications leading to crews orbiting the target for a long while which allowed the German fighters to catch them while they were concentrated in the target area. The highest casualty rate was amongst 1 Group who formed the second wave, 5 Group faired better, and 619 Squadron lost only one aircraft, that of Plt Offr Wadsworth DFC. The crew was very experienced-there were no less than three DFMs amongst them- but it was an unequal fight and they were shot down near the village of Courbin, some 10 kilometers South East of Chateau Thierry. All were killed and they are buried in the cemetery of Courbin.

On the 4th May John took his crew on two special bombing practices at Wainfleet, the first at 1500hrs and the second at 2000hrs, both flights lasted about 1h30m. John was anxious to perfect the bombing run, and although Teddy Booth was an experienced air bomber John was thinking ahead to the time that he might be asked to become a marker, and marking required special accuracy.

The weather in the next two days was very bad and there were no operations. Some aircraft flew on air tests but most of the crews attended lectures on escape and evasion and how to resist interrogation if made POW.

Operations were again planned for the night of the 7th May. The target was in the heart of France near a small town called Salbris. John took his crew once again to the bombing ranges for more practice before the usual briefing.

Leaving for a moment the atmosphere of the airfield the reader should perhaps be made aware of some background information on Salbris. There were several important ammunition dumps and factories which the Allies were anxious to destroy before the landings in Normandy. Close to Salbris there existed a large factory, which was under the watchful eye of the French Resistance, and was known to be making thousands of shells for the German Army. Munitions made here were partly stored in a large dump, l'Arsenal de Michenon, rather closer to Salbris itself. The factory, known to the locals as L'Atelier de Chargement, or Camp de Michenon, was under the direction of a German Company, Erhmann Wuhle. Over 2,900 workers were employed in the production of shells of all calibres. The local resistance, lead by an SOE agent, St Paul (Philippe de Vomecourt) and Antoine Vincent, an engineer, reported regularly on the work of the factory. On the 6th May several trains arrived in the rail sidings of the ammunition dump and the Germans began loading some wagons. It was a good sabotage target, but, because of the proximity of Salbris, it was feared that there would be many reprisals in the town. St Paul had his young wireless operator, Muriel Byck, who had only recently arrived from London, send a message to London that an important convoy was about to leave Salbris, perhaps for the Atlantic Wall or the Eastern Front. An answer came back from London straight away to the effect that an air operation was planned for the night of 7/8 May. That night was chosen because, being a Sunday, there would be few French workers in the complex. To stop the train moving away before the bombing could take place the resistance blew the rail lines to the North and South of Salbris, thus trapping the trains ! At HQ Bomber Command no time was lost in ordering the raid which,because it was a precision target, was allocated to 5 Group which was gaining experience in low level marking.. A message was sent to St Paul informing him that the attack was imminent.. On the 7th May a message was received via the BBC- "L'eau sale brille".-The dirty water shines !

At Conningsby there was much to do. 83, 97 and 627 Squadrons had three targets to mark,-Nantes, Tours and Salbris, would there be enough aircraft to cover all three targets ?.At Metheringham, Conningsby, Fiskerton, Woodhall Spa and Dunholme Lodge the ground crews were hard at work to make sure that the maximum number of aircraft would be ready for take off. These unsung heroes gave everything and their only reward was to see their crews return safely. They knew that the lives of the aircrews depended on their vigilance and dedication, and although their work was not as dangerous they worked long hours, sometimes in terrible conditions, rain, cold winds and with snow on their boots; their worst nightmare was to find an empty dispersal on the following morning and the realization that their aircrew had "had it". Many of them longed to get in the air, and they dreamed of earning a coveted flying badge- if only to attract the local girls, but without their work on the ground many more crews and aircraft would have failed to return.

John was to be the Master Bomber on this raid, particular attention was paid to the radio,- communications had to be perfect. As darkness fell the muffled sound of engines pervaded the Lincolnshire air. At each base great engines were started up, first coughing and belching smoke then settling down into that steady purr that was instantly recognizable as a Merlin engine. "Chocks away", one by one the great birds left their dispersal areas and lined up ready for the signal to take off. Heavily loaded the aircraft appeared to waddle on strained undercarriages as they made their way around the perimeter tracks. WAAFs and ground crews were there to see their friends off, as brakes were released they gave a cheery wave, perhaps even a silent prayer, in the hope that all on board would make a safe return.

Target for tonight? Crew briefing

The moment of truth. The Station Commander and ground crew give an encouraging wave, and perhaps a silent prayer, as a Halifax bomber prepares to take off on a raid. *IWM Photos*

The weather was good that night, some moonlight and only a few clouds. The course was easy-Reading- Selsey Bill, over the French coast near Cabourg and then direct to Salbris all at a height of 5,000ft. Soon after the start John noticed a Lancaster pulling out of the stream, it turned slowly to port loosing some height as it did so. It was from 44 Squadron, apparently the mid upper gunner had developed violent ear ache and his captain had decided to return to base, dropping his bombs in the sea. John's flight engineer, "Tuck" Fryer was busy checking all the guages, fuel, oil pressures etc, "Nulli Secundus" was running well as he led the 57 Lancasters to the target. They were not alone that night, Bomber Command had laid on several different attacks in order to confuse the German fighter controllers; other targets included an ammunition dump at Rennes which was attacked by 55 aircraft from 1 Group, the airfields near Tours and Nantes were attacked while a force of Halifax bombers attempted to bomb coastal gun batteries at St Valery. In all 470 heavy bombers ensured that the Germans in France had little sleep. However some German night fighters did make their way to the target areas and twelve heavy bombers did not return. Near Chateaudun a Lancaster of 106 Squadron tried vainly to escape from a night fighter. On fire, the pilot Cyril Bartlett, gave the order to release the bombs in the hope of gaining some speed and manoeuvrability and if possible make a crash landing, but the fighter hung on and after taking many hits and making some violent turns the aircraft broke in two. Three of the crew fell with the tail section and were killed instantly, the other part of the bomber fell some distance away. The mid upper gunner was thown out of the wreck and died later having lost an arm, the others died in the fireball, it was their 14th operation. In another fighter attack the results were much the same. Sqn Ldr Hunter in a 44 Squadron Lancaster lost the unequal battle with a fighter and with both wings on fire gave the order to bale out, but before the crew got away the fire reached the fuel tanks and the aircraft blew up in a great shower of metal, flame and black smoke. Only the flight engineer survived, he was blown clear and his parachute opened saving his life, he became a POW. All the others perished although, in spite of the enormous blast as the bombs exploded, only the pilot's body was mutilated, the others were found intact, one body was found sitting with his back to a tree as if just waiting for someone .The blast from the bombs blew a hole 30meters wide by 8 meters deep and the nearby village of Herbilly was virtually destroyed, luckily only seven civilians were killed.

The Illuminators of 83 Squadron identified the factory and the ammunition dump and released a carpet of flares. The few watchmen at the factory were filled with wonder by the spectacle. With the targets well lit up the Mosquitoes of 627 Squadron made their low level marking runs. Fg Offr Saint-Smith was the first to mark the aiming point on the factory. His red spot fires fell right on the roof of the store shed- "bang on". A fire started immediately.

In the factory a young worker who was on duty at the infirmary witnessed the marking;- "It was very beautiful, the sky was so bright in the light of the flares that it was like daytime. I clearly saw a small plane which dived on us, he was so low I thought he was going to land on the factory!, something dropped from the aircraft and exploded. I ran to the shelter". The marker leader, Sqn Ldr Mackensie, called John on the VHF to tell him that the marking was good and in turn John called in the main force to aim at the red spot fires. A deluge of bombs then fell on the buildings and the markers became obscured by the smoke, the Lancasters of 83 Squadron backed up with new red spots fires.

The ammunition dump to the North East was marked with green spot fires released by Fg Offr Thompson, a New Zealander. This target was exclusive to 106 Squadron. For John the mission went smoothly, almost like an exercise, even the radio worked well for a change. The Lancasters made their bomb runs releasing their 4,000 lb "Cookies" and 500lb bombs with great precision, and John had only a few corrections to transmit, whilst orbiting he thought he saw an enemy fighter in the light of the fires but it did not attack. The explosions were so great that all aircraft felt the blast. One massive explosion shook the bomber like a wisp of straw. The crew saw one Lancaster in flames, first looking like a flare dropping horizontally, then diving slowly it hit the ground and exploded in a great ball of orange and red flame. John's navigator, Gosling, remarked - "they got the chop". It was an aircraft of 106 Squadron piloted by a Canadian, Plt Offr H.K. Rose. They had no time to release the bombs and only the bomb aimer, John Smith, had time to jump to safety, the others going down trapped in the aircraft by centrifugal force. Smith landed safely not far from the crash site , and was quickly gathered up by some French helpers who, almost under the noses of the Germans who had also been looking for him, stripped him of his uniform, gave him a jacket and French beret, burnt his parachute in the fire caused when the bomber crashed, and drove him off on the back of a motor bike. A few hundred meters up the road they were stopped by some German soldiers, but the driver, with typical French sangfroid, told the soldiers that he had seen an airman running in the opposite direction, the soldiers set off in hot pursuit- chasing shadows !

The German night fighters arrived in force as the bombers were leaving the target area and they quickly shot down three bombers. The first to go was Lancaster JB 421 of 49 Squadron, the crew were on their first operation, the aircraft blew up and was scattered near some woods by the village of Souesmes, all were killed. The second aircraft crashed in flames not far from the first, it was an aircraft from 106 Squadron piloted by an Australian. Just before the crash the plane was seen to avoid a chateau. A local farmer ran to try and help but it was hopeless, the crew were all dead, most badly mutilated by the force of the crash and explosion, one woman helper fainted in horror when she discovered a leg in a tree. The third Lancaster, again from 106 Squadron fell victim to a night fighter and fell near Loreux, ten kilometers from the target. The tail section landed on the outskirts of the village and the main part in a nearby field. The crew were one of the most experienced on the squadron and had returned from the disastrous Nurenbourg raid, making an emergency landing at Manston where there were no serious casualties but their aircraft had been written off, this night however their luck had run out. The 619 Squadron aircraft had followed each other over the target from about 0025 to 0036 hrs. All crews reported the massive explosion at 0026hrs, with smoke and flames ascending to 6,000ft, one aircraft from 83 Squadron had felt the force of the explosion some eight kilometers from the factory. Lancaster ND 517 was hit by flak and after landing the crew discovered 24 holes in the port wing, the rudder controls were almost severed, the fuselage holed and the intercom was unserviceable. Sqn Ldr Whamond, one of John's Flight Commanders, was hit before he got to the target, he feathered the port outer engine at 0022hrs and pressed on to drop his bombs at 0032hrs. Flt Sgt Paterson was attacked twice by fighters, his rear gunner returned fire and claimed to have hit the enemy. As he was pulling away from the target John was able to see that an electric power station to the South of the target had been completely destroyed.

It had been a bad night for 106 Squadron, their target, the ammunition dump, was very scattered with no precise aiming point. Plt Offr Brodie saw his bombs miss the target, Wg Cdr Piercy did better and saw some bunkers blow up, Bellingham went in very low in order to avoid the German night fighters but risking the blast from his own bombs, in fact he was so low he hit some pylons and lost his H2S!. But worst of all the squadron had lost four out of the twelve aircraft sent on the raid. John made a final orbit of the target and, satisfied with the results, called to the main force- "good prang boys- now go home", and then over the intercom to his crew- "Leslie and Jack keep your eyes open there are many Huns about tonight." It was a long trip home via the Cherbourg peninsular and then across the English Channel to Portland, and there was one more bomber lost, that of Sqn Ldr Fred Fuller, which came down near Champigny en Beauce to the North of Blois, all the crew were killed. Nor was it easy for John and his crew, Jack Howard the rear gunner spotted a Dornier 217 below and to starboard, he warned John and the mid upper gunner Les Birch, both gunners fired and the Dornier broke away with his port engine and cockpit in flames,- "Well done boys" shouted John, but a little later Alec Bates, the radio operator, told John he thought they had been hit, John accused him of an over active imagination but as we will see Alec had been right.

They landed safely at their base and there was no further talk of having been hit, but the following morning Alec Bates recalls- "I went out to do my DI but "Nulli Secundus" was not at her dispersal. On enquiring the chief technician told me she was in the hangar and was Cat C-repairable on site but by the manufacturers only. I cycled back to the Flight Office and met some of the crew who said *have you heard?* I said I had and then asked what the "old man" had said- they replied he had said young Alec is vindicated". Apparently "Nulli Secundus" had been hit by some very light flak during one of the low passes over the target, fortunately no vital part of the aircraft had been damaged.

It was just after his discussion with the crew that Alec learnt that Sqn Ldr Fuller's aircraft was missing. This was a sad blow to Alec as the wireless operator was his friend John Hill.Again Alec recalls- "John was an electrician by trade and had been in charge of re-wiring our home in 1937-the year I left school, and we had become good friends.As soon as I could I went to see John's parents, not an easy experience,- what can one say ?"

While their aircraft was being repaired the crew were stood down but an operation involving the squadron was ordered for the 9th May. The target was the aircraft factory at Genevilliers, a Gnome et Rhone company. Twelve aircraft from 619 Squadron took off but one returned early, Fg Offr Baker having trouble with his starboard outer engine.One squadron aircraft was lost, that of Plt Offr Aitken who was carrying a second pilot Flt Sgt Goodwin.

Salbris 8th May 1944. The steam plant after some attention by
No 5 Group Bomber Command.

Salbris. The morning after. A general view.
Photos via Alain Charpentier

On the 11th May "Nulli Secundus" was again serviceable and John took her up for some fighter affiliation training, the last encounter with the Dornier had left John feeling a little uneasy about their tactics. An operation was planned for that night, this time 15 Lancasters from 619 Squadron formed part of a force of 190 heavy bombers and eight Mosquitos ordered to bomb the German military depot at Bourg Leopold in Belgium. The depot was similar to Mailly le Camp, used for training and re-equiping German army units. The raid was a failure, first of all John had to turn back with problems in his starboard outer engine which blew a radiator hose, igniting some glycol. The automatic fire extinguisher soon had the fire out but the engine had to be shut down and it was hopeless trying to keep up with the others on three engines. For the remainder the weather was bad and there were troubles with the target marking, part of the main force started bombing the nearby village of Beverlo by mistake and efforts by the Master Bomber to stop the bombing were not successful. Only six aircraft from 619 Squadron bombed, the others returned to base without bombing. Five Lancasters from the main force were lost but the greater tragedy occurred on the ground where the village of Beverlo was virtually destroyed and 84 civilians were killed.

The next morning John's ground crew were anxious to discover the reason for the early return. They discovered that the hose had been damaged during the previous encounter with the Dornier and the fitter who had made the earlier inspection was charged with neglect. John dismissed the case with the words "he would have needed X-Ray eyes to have found it"

On the 13th May the aircraft was again serviceable, further checks were made and John took off on yet more bombing practice. Later he went off to RAF Manby where special courses were being run for future Master Bombers. It was also at this time that he learnt that he had been awarded an immediate DFC and was being posted to Coningsby as a Controller, both events costing him a few beers in the Officers and NCOs messes.

John was sad to leave his squadron after six months of intensive operations, he had made many friends and earned the respect of all members; he was however taking most of his crew with him as they were transferred to 83 (PFF) Squadron at Coningsby. As has already been written, that squadron was transferred, after much argument, from AVM Bennet's Pathfinder Group to the special marking force set up by AVM Cochrane. This special force was under command of Air Commodore Sharp,the commander of 54 Base, which comprised the RAF stations of Coningsby and Woodhall Spa.

On the 15th May John officially handed over 619 Squadron to Sqn Ldr Wharmond, one of the flight commanders, as the new Wing Commander had not yet arrived. His last flight in "Nulli Secundus" was to Dunholme, and it was on that flight that his crew, for the first and only time, became apprehensive about his handling of the aircraft, John did not appear to be his normally controlled self as he made a very low pass over the control tower as a gesture of "farewell".

On the 18th May John arrived at Coningsby and took over a new aircraft, Lancaster ND 840 which was on the strength of 83 (PFF) Squadron. The aircraft had been specially fitted for use by the Master Bombers, or Controllers as they became known, in the 5 Group Special Marking Force. Two other Controllers arrived at the same time, Wg Cdr Tait from 83 Base, and Acting Wg Cdr Simpson from 97 (PFF) Squadron. The special crews involved in the new force had been transferred so quickly that there was an initial shortage of accommodation, flying rations and escape packs; John, with his, now legendary, ability to get things done, spoke to the Station Commander, Group Captain Evans-Evans, and soon had these problems sorted out.

One of John's original crew members, Wireless operator Alec Bates, has provided further insight into John's sense of duty towards his crews, and to his attitude to operational flying. Alec Bates has written- " He was very kind to me, often teasing me

116

because I did not drink, and calling me his dehydrated wireless operator. At the time I was infatuated with a young woman in the Women's Land Army. One day as I was walking towards Coningsby the skipper came by in his old Rover car and gave me a lift. On the way he asked *-are you going to marry that girl ?*, no sir I replied its all over - *good I'm glad to hear it because if you were you would have been out of my crew-* I protested- but sir, Teddy (the bomb aimer) is married- *yes* he replied , *but he has been married for years and has had time to get over it !, I don't want you mooning about some female when you should be concentrating on an operation.*"

On the 19th May plans were made for yet another attack on the railway yards at Tours. This was to be John's first time as controller since his move to 54 Base. The plan for the attack was that the target would be illuminated by flares dropped by 83 (PFF) Squadron, by the light of which Mosquitoes from 627 Squadron would dive and place red spot markers on the aiming points and these would be cancelled or supplemented by the controller. There were also some fairly complicated instructions regarding the use of offset markers and the release of bombs, the latter designed to produce a pattern of bombs with 20 yards between craters.The Base Commander and AVM Cochrane made a special point of attending the briefing, explaining that it was necessary to destroy the rail facilities at Tours in order to slow down the German's ability to reinforce their forces when the Allied invasion began; they also emphasised that extreme accuracy in bombing was needed in order to minimise casualties amongst the French civilian population living near the target area.

With the briefing over John went over the details with his crew, which now had some new members. Flt Sgt Lawes became the flight engineer, Fg Offr Cooper replaced Booth as the bomb aimer and an additional navigator, Fg Offr Kemp, to work with Gosling and operate the H2S radar. During the afternoon the weather was bad and there was talk of cancelling the operation but

117

a better forecast for the target area resulted in the decision to go.In an attempt to confuse the German night fighter controllers it had been decided to mount multiple attacks on the French rail targets, and altogether some 900 aircraft took to the skies above Eastern England that night.

For John's particular effort the Lancasters began taking off at 2200hrs, the weather at the time was poor but it did improve as they crossed over the Channel between Seaford and the French coast at Fecamp. The first flare went down sometime after 0036 hrs-eight and a half minutes before the Zero Hour. Two Mosquitoes from 627 Squadron dived and put their markers down about 500 yards West of the aiming points. Wg Cdr Tait, the nominated Controller was having trouble with his VHF radio, and could not pass on the wind information to the main force crews waiting to set their bombsights. Tait handed control over to John who instructed his navigator to work out the wind quickly, but then he too had radio trouble and there was some delay in passing the vital information on to the waiting crews, and most crews claimed that they did not receive the wind information until after Zero Hour, in fact the first bombs went down four minutes late at 0049hrs, the rate of bombing reached a peak two minutes later. John's assessment of the bombing was that it was well concentrated around the Northern aiming point but there was some overshooting at the Southern one. At 0102 hrs John was no longer able to asses the accuracy due to smoke and cloud and he gave the order to stop bombing. From start to finish the attack had lasted 26 minutes, during which time some 1,300 bombs had been dropped-almost one per second.

On the ground at Tours the air raid sirens sounded as the first flares dropped and people took to their shelters. In the actual railway station there was some panic because a train was in the process of being unloaded with refugees from Rouen, which had been bombed that morning by the USAAF. A number of bombs fell wide resulting in some 1,300 houses being damaged or destroyed and 137 French civilians were killed. Back in the air there were a number of minor collisions and near misses, but all the aircraft were able to struggle homeward without interference from the German night fighters which had been confused by the multiple attacks

Returning to their bases the crews were faced with deteriorating weather and there were many diversions. One aircraft, flown by Plt Offr Irving from 50 Squadron, crashed on the approach to Benson in Oxfordshire, killing the pilot, navigator and bomb aimer.

It was several days before air photos could be obtained, but eventually the photo interpreters were able to confirm that the main targets, the locomotive depot and workshops, had been severely damaged and that the main lines to Saumur and Poitiers had been cut. However it was not possible for the Intelligence Staffs to write the target off their list, and it was not until a further raid after the D Day landings that Tours was finally regarded as impassable by German troop trains trying to reach the Normandy area.

Three nights later an operation was planned against Brunswick. John was nominated as the main controller, this time of a slightly larger force of 225 Lancasters from 1 and 5 Groups. Low level marking was to be carried out by ten Mosquitoes, but in spite of a good forecast the weather over the target was bad, and they were unable to carry out their mission. In addition John experienced once again problems with his VHF radio and neither he nor his deputy,Wg Cdr Northrop, could give any clear instructions. As a result most of the bombs fell in open country and the raid was termed a failure. Worse still, the delay in trying to identify the target had given the German night fighters time to assemble and find the bomber stream, thirteen of which were shot down- 5.5% of the force, -an unacceptably high loss rate.

On the 27th May the 5 Group markers and controllers were split between heavy gun batteries on the French coast and the railway junction at Nantes. John, in Lancaster "A" from 83 (PFF)

Squadron, was the controller for the attacks on the gun battery at Morsalines, while Wg Cdr Tait controlled the raid on Nantes. The 155mm guns of the Morsalines battery were not yet encased-due to chaos imposed on the French railway system by the "Transportation Plan" which, in this case, had delayed deliveries of cement. The raid was moderately successful, in that the Germans felt obliged to move the battery further inland, and it did not appear to be in operation at the time of the invasion on the 5/6th June. But for John it was another frustration, with radio problems once again forcing him to hand over control to his deputy, and, being unable to identify the target clearly he had no alternative but to take his bombs back to England. On his return to 54 Base he sought a meeting with the Base Commander and AVM Cochrane in order to explain his problems and make suggestions for the future. As a result John flew in an Oxford trainer down to Stanmore, the home of the Bomber Command radio school. Here he spent two day discussing radio procedures and ways of overcoming his problems.

On the **1st June** John led 50 aircraft of 5 Group, including ten from 83 (PFF) Squadron, to illuminate mark and control a small raid on the railway junction at Saumur-(close to the tunnel made famous by 617 Squadron when they blocked it using 12,000 pound "Tallboy" bombs shortly after D Day). His aircraft this time was Lancaster NE 167, on loan from 97 (PFF) Squadron, and was fitted with the new Stabilized Automatic Bomb Site (SABS) and carried the Mk 3 version of the H2S radar which had a much improved definition. Only three aicraft of 5 Group had been fitted with the new equipment at this time and all were for use by Master Bombers. As usual John took his aircraft on a test flight during the afternoon in order familiarize his crew with the new equipment.

They took off for Saumur at 2230hrs. It was the second attack on the town in two days. The previous raid by 82 Lancasters and four Mosquitoes of 5 Group had been moderately successful but the planners required that the railway lines and bridge over the Loire should be completely blocked. This time the target was

120

marked by 83(PFF) Squadron Lancasters and no Mosquitoes were involved. The raid was very successful and much damage was done.

All the operations by 5 Group in the next few days were connected with the forthcoming Allied invasion of Normandy. While all this was going on John asked Air Commodore Sharp if he could start using a Mosquito aircraft for marking targets and controlling the attacks. The Air Commodore agreed and John went over to 627 Squadron at Woodhall Spa for some flying instruction. At Woodhall he was assigned an "instructor" and they took up Mosquito DZ 516 , first with John sitting in the navigators seat and then with him in the customary left hand seat at the controls.Being rather tall he found things rather cramped compared to his Lancaster, and being at the controls of a twin engined aircraft once again brought back memories of Blenheims and Baltimores, and all the men in his previous squadrons. Opening the throttles he was amazed at the power generated by the two Merlin engines, and at first had to be cautioned by his instructor to "take it easy" when taxying. But he quickly got the hang of things and was soon putting the aircraft through its paces. He found the aircraft very responsive and a joy to fly after the heavy Lancasters. After landing and parking the aircraft his 627 Squadron pilot remarked " you seem to be very experienced on twin engined types" and it was only then that John divulged his operational experience in Blenheims and Baltimores.

The next day John asked Jack Howard , the rear gunner of his Lancaster crew, to ride as a passenger with him in a Mosquito to the bombing range at Wainfleet. Together they spent some 50 minutes in the air while John tried his bombing techniques using practice bombs in place of the red spot fires which he was to use in later target marking operations.At first his aim was not all that good but it improved.

On the 5th June, the night prior to D Day, John was given the job of controlling a small raid on the coast defence guns at La

Pernelle. 5 Group had three tasks that night, La Pernelle, St Pierre du Mont and the special operation "Taxable" by 617 Squadron, which was designed to simulate a large fleet of ships heading towards Cap D`Antifer on the French coast. At the usual briefing an officer from Group HQ announced that "This is it-D Day", all the operations were in support of the invasion, the attacks on the coast defence guns were to silence the guns threatening the ships carrying the troops to the beaches. The weather over Normandy was bad, and John was lucky to spot a gap in the cloud sheet. Diving through it he began to control the attack, but once again communications were not too good and some of the main force of bombers did not respond to his orders, with the result that the bombing became rather scattered, in the end John called a halt to the bombing with the words " you can go home now you cannot bomb for toffee". On the way home the crews were able to see the mass of shipping making its way towards the Normandy beaches,-a moving sight that none could forget. Having been de-briefed after landing most of the crews did not go to bed as usual but stayed up listening to news of the invasion on the BBC radio.

Later that day John was again practising his flying of a Mosquito, this time with his regular navigator Len Gosling. Gosling quickly adapted to the cramped conditions and lack of a proper navigation table afforded by the navigator`s seat alongside his skipper.

From D Day onwards RAF Bomber Command and the heavy bombers of the 8th USAAF were used in an increasingly tactical capacity, supplementing the efforts of the fighter bombers of the 2nd Tactical Air Force. By day any German troop movements triggered attacks by fighters and medium bombers and by night Bomber Command attacked the road and rail "choke points" as the Germans strove to reinforce their hard pressed formations on the Normandy battlefield. It is to their everlasting credit that the French civilians withstood the inevitable casualties in the interests of their liberation.

John's first operation as a Controller using a Mosquito came on the night of the 8/9th June against the railway junction at Pontaubault. The aircraft was a Mk IV version, serial DZ 521 and carrying the code letters AZ-M from No 627 Squadron. He and the navigator from his old Lancaster crew, Les Gosling, took off at 2305hrs and arrived over the target at 0035hrs. One of their markers fell well short of the aiming point and had to be cancelled by John's Deputy, Wg Cdr Dean. Ten minutes later the main force was ordered to bomb. Much damage was caused and the raid was judged successful.

The next afternoon John took a Lancaster on a flight test, but was later briefed to become the Controller for an attack on the rail yards at Etampes and he decided to use the Mosquito he had flown the previous night. The target was closely surrounded by civilian housing and once again there were many casualties amongst the civilian population. Nor was it a particularly successful raid, John's marking was accurate enough but rather late and six of the 108 Lancasters taking part were shot down. It appears that John was once again having trouble with his radio procedures. On the 11th June he took his radio operator Alec Bates up in the Mosquito with the intention of getting him to put in a report, saying that the radio was unserviceable. He said to Alec- "The set is useless." Alec duly filed his report and the set was replaced.

On the 12/13th June John and Len Gosling set out in the same Mosquito to control a raid on Caen, which was being stubbornly held by the German army. Luck evaded them once again, this time the port engine failed and John handed over control once more. Landing back safely at Coningsby on one engine did however show that not all his luck had run out, and it gave him extra confidence in the Mosquito. The bombing of Caen on this occasion was however very scattered and much damage was done to the city, which was later to prove a hinderance to Allied troops trying to negotiate all the rubble.

On the 14th June John appears to have made his last flight in a Lancaster with his old crew from No 619 Squadron. Flying in JB 309, coded "N" of No 83 (PFF) Sqn, they were towing a target for fighter affiliation training. That night he was once again on operations. The target was an area around the small town of Aunay sur Odon and the operation was mounted in great haste having been especially requested by the army. Apparently reports had been received that the Germans were concentrating a large number of tanks in the area, thus posing a serious threat to the Allied bridgehead near Caen. John, with other Mosquitoes from No 627 Squadron, carried out the marking while Wg Cdr Northrop acted as Controller. The concentration of bombs released by the Lancasters and Halifax aircraft taking part was remarkable and was described by General Bayerlein, commander of the Panzer Lehr Division, as devasting. Apparently some 70% of his division were either killed, wounded or just numbed by the bombing which completely destroyed all the forward tank units. It was later reported that General Witt, commander of the 12th SS Panzer Division was killed in the attack.

On the 21st June, after a slight pause in operations due to the weather, and with slow progress by the Allied ground forces, Bomber Command turned their attention to the synthetic oil refineries in Germany. No 5 Group were ordered to two of these plants, Wesseling amd Gelsenkirchen. John and Wg Cdr Tait were the controllers, John for Gelsenkirchen and Tait for Wesseling. This proved to be a lucky choice for John because although the casualties at Gelsenkirchen were high-6%- those at Wesseling were a staggering 27.8% - 37 bombers out of a force of 133, including six Lancasters from John's old Squadron - 619. In the event Gelsenkirchen turned out to be cloud covered and low level marking was replaced by four Pathfinder Mosquitoes dropping Sky Markers with the aid of OBOE. Unable to effectively control the attack John headed for home. Back at Coningsby three very experienced Pathinder crews were missing, two from No 83 Squadron and one from 97 Squadron.

In spite of many earlier air attacks on the German V weapons launching sites in the Pas de Calais the night of 12/13th June 1944 saw the first V1 "Flying Bombs" fall on England. On the 18th June a V1 fell on the Guards Chapel close to Buckingham Palace, killing over 100 people and from thereon the German V1 offensive increased to a point where the British government became greatly concerned for the safety and morale of the population living in the London area and the South of England. Defensive measures were hastily organised, fighter tactics amended and anti-aircraft guns moved to form defensive belts from the channel to the London area. However the Allied commanders in Normandy were more concerned with the possibility of the new German weapons being targeted against the ports and shipping which were vital to the build up of the Normandy beach head. Bomber Command was once again asked to divert its attention to the destruction of the V1 and V2 rocket sites in North West France.

Bad weather prevented an immediate and substantial response, but on the night of the 24/25th June a total of 535 Lancaster and 165 Halifax bombers from Bomber Command attacked seven V1 sites. No 5 Group had two targets, Prouville and Pommervale. John, flying a Mosquito from No. 627 Squadron, controlled the attack on the Prouville sites which was well cratered. This was to be his last fully successful operation as a controller, two days later he was given the job of Base Operations Officer and his place was taken by Wg Cdr J. Woodroffe from No 61 Squadron.

At this time Air Cdre Sharp and Wg Cdr Cheshire were experimenting with American single seat fighters for use by Marker Leaders and Master Bombers. Using his previous contacts with the USAAF Sharp managed to borrow two P51 Mustangs and one P38 twin boomed Lightning fighters. Cheshire had some success with the Mustang and John was asked to try out the Lightning. After some training on the range at Wainfleet John was given the task of controlling a small raid on the rail yards at Villeneuve, to the South West of Paris. It had been many years since John had been in a single seat aircraft and never in a modern high speed one, as a result he became "unsure of his position" and well to the South of Paris. Realising his mistake he made a radio call to his deputy, instructing him to carry on with the attack. By the time John reached the target area the raid was well under way and, feeling somewhat ashamed of himself, he decided to head for home. Back at Coningsby he spent the next few days making practise bombing runs with the Lightning. The 54 Base monthly Newsletter "Gen" notes that he and his Base Commander A/Cdre Sharp, had a competition and that "the two Lockheed Lightning experts Sharp and Jeudwine were averaging 9 and 9.5 yards error in practise bombing runs for target marking."

While all this was going on John's old crew from 619 Squadron, less Jack Howard, were posted to 617 Squadron, their new pilot being Sqn Ldr John Cockshot. Jack Howard became the Base Gunnery Leader at Coningsby. A little later 619 Squadron was to receive another severe blow to morale when they lost five of 13 aircraft taking part in another raid on the rail yards at Revigny.It is not quite clear from the records whether John was using the Lightning or a Mosquito on this raid, but he was the Master Bomber. The raid was rather a shambles, due at first to the fact that five Lancasters had been shot down in the target area and some crews had mistaken fires from the crashed aircraft as the markers John ordered a delay of five minutes while the markers were re-laid. Later, having given the order "bomb on the fires" he amended the order to bomb on the one remaining Red Spot marker. During the confusion the German night fighters had caught up with the bombers and shot down 24 Lancasters- 22% of the total force. It was John's least successful operation. On the 5th August John was promoted and posted as Station Commander of RAF

Most of Jeudwine's Lancaster crew, after he had left 619 Sqn and they had a new pilot.
Standing: L to R. Les Birch Rear Gunner, Geoff Bradbury Mid Upper Gunner,
John Cockshot Pilot, Len Gosling Navigator, Bob Fryer Flight Engineer.
Kneeling: L to R. Ted Booth Bomb Aimer, Alec Bates Wireless op.

Aircraft used in Control and Low Level Marking

De Havilland Mosquito. Crew two

P38 Lightning. Single seat. Jeudwine did not have much
success with this as he was unused to pilot navigation in high
speed aircraft

Dunholme Lodge. His place was taken by Wg Cdr Guy Gibson of "Dambusters" fame.

At Dunholme he met up once again with No 619 Squadron. The new CO was Wg Cdr Robert Milward, a very experienced officer with a background similar to John's in that he had commanded No 30 Squadron in the Middle East and No 67 Squadron in the Far East. Milward recalls:- "I knew Jeudwine first at Dunholme and then at Strubby. As a previous CO he took great interest in the squadron- almost to the point of relegating me to a Flight Commander ! However this problem never reached a state whereby it affected our friendship and we flew together on several occasions. The Group held bombing competitions to bring home the importance of the relationship between bomb aimers and pilots, and we sometimes took it in turns to be the bomb aimer while the other flew the aircraft. Jeudwine was a very close and uncommunicating person, and spoke rarely of his private life, I do not even know if he was married, all his conversation was about the strategy and tactics of heavy bomber operations."

The summer of 1944 brought the breakout from the Normandy beach heads and the gradual liberation of much of France. On September 17th John had the opportunity of flying with A/Cdre Pope, Commander of 52 Base, as observers during a heavy attack on German troop positions around Boulogne. Two nights later came the sad news that Wg Cdr Gibson had been killed whilst returning from the control of a raid on Munchengladbach in Germany. The aircraft, a Mosquito from 627 Squadron, had crashed in Holland.

At the end of September No 619 Squadron was moved to RAF Strubby and John followed them there as Station Commander. He was to remain at Strubby until August 1945 when the station became a Maintenance Unit. At Strubby John preferred to keep his eye on the operational side. A 619 Squadron pilot John Whiteley recalls:- " Group Captain Jeudwine often mixed with the air crews and I spoke to him on several occasions, but I cannot claim to have known him well. He was a popular Station Commander, very experienced but never domineering over the junior officers, who he always encouraged and supported. I once returned from a daylight raid on the Ruhr and he was in the control tower. My landing was not the best I ever made in a Lancaster and over a drink in the mess he pulled my leg about the ropey landing. In a fit of bravado I challenged him to a landing competition to be judged by the squadron commander. I have to admit he won and it cost me a round of drinks."

John certainly appears to have been more a man of action, and to have disliked the administrative side of being a station commander with all its problems of security, messing and discipline and, as Wg Cdr Milward remarked - " he was only really happy when he had his hands on the controls of an aeroplane".

The winter of 1944/45 was bad, but apart from the set back caused by Von Runstedt's Ardennes offensive the Allies gradually reached and crossed the Rhine into Germany. In April 1945, as the war in Europe was drawing to a close, it became apparent that a large number of people in Holland were seriously short of food. Bomber Command rose to the occasion by mounting operation "Manna", and Lancasters were used to transport and drop some six and a half thousand tons of food. Altogether Nos 1, 3 and 8 Groups flew nearly 3,000 sorties and without doubt saved many from starvation.

On the 4th May the German army commander visited General Montgomery's Headquarters on Luneburg Heath and signed a document of surrender. On the 7th May General Eisenhower accepted the unconditional surrender of all German forces on all fronts. The war was officially over at midnight on the 8th but the celebrations at RAF bases had already begun. One of the contributors to this book told us of a WAAF running across the room to throw her arms around John and kiss him. Who was she?, we will probably never know, but the incident was one of many signs of jubilation and relief that the "chop nights" were over.

Since their formation in April 1943 No 619 Squadron had flown over 3,000 sorties, taken part in 223 bombing raids and had lost 77 aircraft on operations and another 12 in accidents.

At Strubby John and his old squadron became involved in the repatriation of British Prisoners of War who had been liberated from their camps in Germany. Known as operation "Exodus", Lancasters from Nos 1,5,6 and 8 Groups were tasked with flying to airfields in France and Belgium where they picked up the former POWs and brought them back to some 25 different airfields in England. Each Lancaster was capable of carrying up to 25 passengers and John and 619 Squadron were much involved. On the 2nd May John flew with the new CO of 619 Squadron to Lille where they made arrangements for the pick ups. Later that day John returned to Lille with a maintenance crew. Their passengers were deposited at Westcott airfield.

With the war in Europe well and truly over John encouraged pilots from Strubby to take part in the "Cooks Tour" operation, -taking ground crews to see the damage done to the German towns,- many could not believe the devastation. On the 22nd May he organised a party and invited his old crew members. Jack Howard flew in from Abingdon, and John flew him back again three days later-some party ! Sadly it was to be the last time they were together.

John`s friend and former Base Commander A/Cdre Sharp was promoted, and played an important part in the formation and preparations for re-deployment of a Bomber Command force to the Far East. Known as "Tiger" force it was never deployed because in August the two atomic bombs were dropped on Japan and the war there came to an abrupt end.

In July 1945 No 619 Squadron was disbanded, and in August, as RAF Strubby was on the point of closing down, John was posted as Station Commander to Little Staughton, an 8(PFF) Group station. He had a short leave and visited his mother and sister, who by then had a baby daughter-now Nonie Beckingsale who has helped with this story. On the 10th September he took over Little Staughton, with instructions to close the airfield. It was just six weeks before his final flight. During his time with Bomber Command he had flown on 31 operational sorties amounting to some 175 hours. Unfortunately we have been unable to locate his flying log book but a summary of his operational flights with Bomber Command is included in Appendix 2 at the back of this book.

Alain Charpentier. France 1999.

Notes on Chapter 4.

1.Wg Cdr Jeudwine's service record gives 1654 HCU, but this was apparently changed.

2. Many crews had the same experience of losing their original pilots.

3. Fg Offr Day had been with John at the Lancaster Finishing School and had been posted to 619 Sqn at the same time as John.

CHAPTER 5

The Final Flight

At 1255hrs on the 19th October 1945 John took off from Little Staughton Airfield in a single seat Typhoon 1B , for what is believed to have been an air test following a routine inspection of the aircraft. Six minutes later at 1301hrs the aircraft crashed close to the North side of the airfield and John was killed.

The aircraft, serial number JR 390, was one of a total of 600 Typhoons under contract number ACFT/943/c/23(a) by the Gloster Aircraft Company at Hucclecote. For part of its service life JR 390 was on the strength of No 183 (Goldcoast) Squadron based at Thorny Island in preparation for the Allied invasion of Normandy in the early part of 1944. The Squadron was later engaged in the ground support role and the Typhoons became known as the "Tank Busters". On the 29th May 1944, bearing the code letters HF-U the aircraft was in the hands of Flying Officer A.R. Taylor when he claimed to have shot down two German Bf 109 fighters some 40 miles South of the Isle of Wight. Sadly, on D Day and following a dog fight near Caen, Taylor , flying a different aircraft, was himself shot down and killed by a Bf 109 .

JR 390 is also believed to have arrived at Little Staughton following VE and VJ Day displays at the nearby towns of St Neots and Bedford.

The official report on the accident, held by The Air Historical Branch of the Ministry of Defence contains the following brief description:-

"Witnesses stated that shortly after take off the aircraft went into a slow roll left then into a spin at 3,000ft from which it did not recover. The accident investigators found no signs of instrument failure and concluded that although a very experienced pilot (2,888 hours), Group Captain Jeudwine had only one hour on type and probably stalled whilst recovering from the inverted position and was unable to recover from the resulting spin".There was an immediate Board of Enquiry set up under the Chairman Group Captain Lawrence from the nearby RAF Station Warboys, and members Wing Commander Grant from RAF Wyton and Flight Lieutenant Pearson from Little Staughton. The medical evidence produced at the enquiry spoke only of multiple injuries. Unfortunately the findings of the court are no longer available, but the Air Historical Branch report was probably based on the general conclusions.

Our own research has produced a little more information:- One witness, Mr Peter Goodridge, a former radio technician based at Little Staughton at the time, saw the aircraft take off and circle the airfield a couple of times, gaining some height.After a short while he "heard the engine cut and heard the crash". Mr Goodridge was one of the first on the scene and described the aircraft lying at a fairly shallow angle between some haystacks, the pilot had been partly scalped by the back of his head having come into contact with the cockpit canopy. Mr Goodridge went on to say that John had left his black and tan Airedale dog in his car (a Hillman Minx) at the aircraft dispersal, and that the dog apparently pined dreadfully for him, but no one seems to remember what happened to the dog.

Another witness, Mr Dennis Pell, who worked for the Air Ministry as an electrician, also remembers the crash- "At about 1300hrs the Typhoon flew low over the control tower so fast that the wing tips were leaving trails, it turned to port, back towards the airfield, then went into a spin from which it did not recover, flying into the ground at a fairly shallow angle under full power." Apparently it was John's second flight, having made an earlier flight from which he returned to report an oil leak. John is reported to have said to the Engineering Officer " there is an oil leak, fix that and I will take it up again and try some aerobatics".The Engineering Officer is believed to have queried the wisdom of this, but John replied "it will handle just like a Hurricane". Mr Pell's version of the dog incident is that a young Flying Officer went to collect John's car and found the dog barking uncontrollably, having probably seen the aircraft crash and sensed that his master was dead.

A few years ago, Chief Technician Peter Stanley, curator of the Pathfinder Museum at RAF Wyton, carried out a recovery operation at the scene of the crash near Crown Farm to the North of the airfield. Unfortunately very little wreckage remained at the site because, due to the shallow impact angle and close proximity to the aerodrome, nearly all had been removed at the time of the accident, but Peter did find some pieces from the cockpit, including a part of John's flying helmet,-perhaps confirming Mr Goodridge's account that the pilot had been partly scalped. Peter Stanley has carried out many such digs and has therefore become experienced in piecing together evidence and making some conclusions. All the items found by Peter were at the lowest part of the dig-some 5 feet down-and from that fact Peter is convinced that the aircraft hit the ground at a shallow angle in the inverted position, which supports the conclusion made in the official report.

A report in a local paper, The Bedfordshire Times and Standard, writes of the pilot's body having been recovered from a position five feet under the aircraft, further supporting the idea that the aircraft crashed upside down. The pieces that Peter found have been mounted onto a board and are on display in the Pathfinder Museum at RAF Wyton.

Finally, in case any reader might pose the question, I feel that it is necessary to refute a rumour that arose from remarks made shortly after the accident by two senior RAF Officers. The rumour suggested that the crash was not entirely an accident. Having carefully examined all the evidence, in particular the fact that the Typhoon was a difficult aircraft requiring a lot of airspace in which to manoeuvre, and having obtained the views of John's contemporaries and subordinates, I am completely satisfied that the crash was a tragic accident, perhaps brought on by over confidence through having flown nearly 3,000 hours in many different types of aircraft from pre-war biplanes to modern fighters and bombers.

L.L-J

The grave in Cambridge cemetery

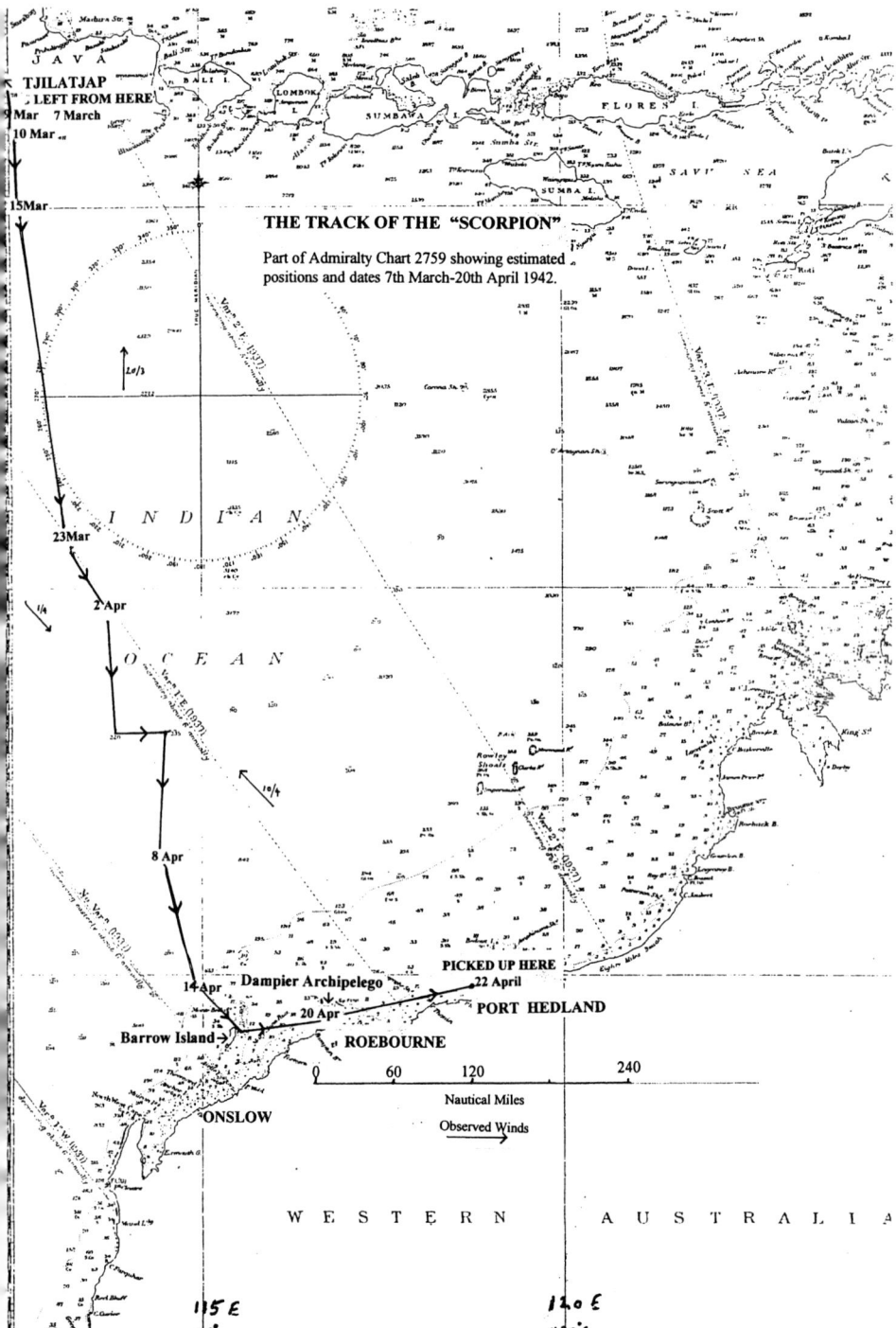

J A V A

TJILATJAP
LEFT FROM HERE
Mar 7 March
10 Mar

BALI I.
LOMBOK
SUMBAW
FLORES I.

SUMBA I.
SAVU SEA

15Mar

THE TRACK OF THE "SCORPION"

Part of Admiralty Chart 2759 showing estimated
positions and dates 7th March-20th April 1942.

I N D I A N

23Mar

2 Apr

O C E A N

8 Apr

14 Apr — Dampier Archipelego
20 Apr
Barrow Island →
ONSLOW

PICKED UP HERE
22 April
PORT HEDLAND
ROEBOURNE

| 0 | 60 | 120 | 240 |

Nautical Miles

Observed Winds

W E S T E R N   A U S T R A L I A

115 E

120 E

138

THE LOG OF THE " SCORPION "

FOREWORD.

No 84 Squadron, Royal Air Force was withdrawn from the Western Desert on 3 January 1942, re-equipped with an increased establishment and sent to the Far East as reinforcements. The squadron operated from Sumatra, Singapore and Java where it lost its remaining aircraft by land attack [1 March 1942]. The ground personnel were left at Bandoeng with the Equipment, Cypher and Engineering Officers while the aircrew were sent to Tjilatjap, a port on the south coast for evacuation.

No ship arrived and the squadron was given the choice of returning inland or making an escape as best they could. An effort was made to escape in two ships lifeboats, all that could be rescued from the fires raging in the port; but this was found to be impractible owing to the crowded state of the boats and personnel were put ashore in a cove, one boat being wrecked in the process.

It was decided that the remaining lifeboat with a crew of twelve should try to reach Australia and get help for the people left behind. The CO and Fg Offr Streatfeild were the only two people who knew anything about sailing. Plt Offr Turner was chosen as Navigator as he could handle a sextant, and Sqn Ldr Passmore was taken as second in command and to look after the rationing. The remainder of the party were chosen from the Australian aircrews as it was felt they should be given a chance of reaching their home country. The crew consisted of;

Wg Cdr J. R. Jeudwine	Captain
Sqn Ldr A. K. Passmore	2 i/c and Purser
Fg Offr C.P.L. Streatfeild	1st Lieutenant and 2nd Helmsman
Plt Offr S. G. Turner	Navigator
Plt Offr M. S. MacDonald	
Sgt G. W. Sayer	

Sgt W. N. Cosgrove
Sgt A. Longmore
Sgt J. Lovegrove
Sgt A.C.E. Snook
Sgt P. M. Corney
Sgt P. Haynes

Personnel remaining behind consisted of three officers and fifty sergeants and aircraftsmen. In addition , four other officers who had come to Tjilatjap [Sqn Ldr Tayler, Flt Lts Wylie and Holland and Fg Offr Owen] were in the vicinity but had become separated from the main party.

Before leaving Tjilatjap a considerable quantity of rations and other foodstuffs had been collected and divided between the boats. Also a quantity of American canned beer had been obtained from a Dutch canteen. This latter undoubtedly largely contributed to the wellbeing of the crew of the "Scorpion" as the water had to be strictly rationed and the beer was a food in itself.

It was calculated that the nearest point on the Australian coast was Roebourne, 950 nautical miles away; with Port Headland and Onslow a little further away to the West and East of the aiming point. It was hoped to cover the distance in 16 days as an illustration in Bartholomews Atlas showed favourable winds and currents at this time of the year, but double this time was allowed for. Some rations were therefore unloaded from the serviceable boat until it was estimated that there was ample food and water for 30 days. Water was contained in three beakers, one full and the others two thirds full, and seven tubs each holding about 12 gallons.

Aids to navigation consisted of a sextant, a 1/15,000,000 Mercators projection of the world, a portion of the Nautical Almanac giving declination tables and time apparent noon, a large scale chart of Java and Bali, and a general navigation chart of the world. [This was not found until land was reached.] There was no chronometer so the C/O's watch was used which was estimated to

2

lose four minutes per day.In view of these preparations, or lack of preparations, the following pages show the enormous luck which attended the "Scorpion " and her crew on their 47 days voyage.

LOG OF HMRAFS "SCORPION"

Tjilatjap to Frazer Islet, 7 March to 20 April 1942

Sat. 7 March

1700   Crew embarked. A very haphazard procedure. Found thirteen people on board so after count had to send Sgt Jeans ashore.

1730   Under way. Boat had to pull out of "Scorpion Cove" as wind was against us.

2300   Heavy thunderstorm and a little wind. Made a few miles SSE. Reverted to oars as soon as wind fell. Navigator, much to his surprise, was sea sick.

Sun.8 March

0800   Rudder came adrift. Damage had been caused by tow rope fouling on night of 6/7. Repair effected by lashing rudder hinge pin with rope. Ration fixed at 10 ozs M&V [meat and veg] or Camp Pie, half a pint of water and four ration biscuits per man per day. If Bully Beef was used ration fell to 9 ozs per day. Cigarettes limited to three per man per day, two good ones and one "good-bad" ie one which had been soaked and dried out.Crew suffering from cramped positions on boat and from sunburn. One or two people got bad burns on their feet. Considerable mental effort required to move about. The hot sun seemed to sap our

3

strength and, although an awning was found and rigged, the heat under it was stifling. Any moving about had to be done on all fours and this in itself was quite an effort.

1615   Breeze from SSW. Made slight Easterly progress.

Mon 9 March

0300   Heavy rain squall which enabled us to collect some water.Becalmed again at 0530 hours.

1200   Position approx. 20 miles SE of Tjilatjap.

1545 Moderate breeze from South West. No sooner had we got under way when a Japanese submarine bearing the marking " 56 " surfaced about a mile astern and steered towards us. She closed to within a 100 yards and we were scrutinised through a pair of binoculars by an officer on the conning tower; one rating standing by a five pounder gun forward and another manning a machine gun on the conning tower. We expected to be shot at or captured, but, after describing a half circle round us the submarine made off towards the East and eventually submerged.This was regarded as a lucky omen. Passed round a can of beer each on sighting the submarine in case we were captured or killed or the submarine turned out to be American and therefore dry.Typical 84 squadron.

1800   Very heavy thunderstorm broke and all water casks fully replenished. Most of the water casks had leaked considerably but they were now soaked enough to hold water. Rain was so heavy that a 12 gallon cask was refilled in half an hour. All members of the crew drank a lot of water which revived them considerably after two days of calm under a bleeding sun. Wind very variable and gusty so hove to. Tot of whisky issued to combat the soaking rain

4

which turned from a blessing to a nuisance. Whisky enabled everyone to sleep in the most extraordinary postures.

Tues. 10 March

0530   Set sail to fresh breeze. Course SSE.

1200   Wind dropped to flat calm. Position approx. 40 miles SE of Tjilatjap. Rudder giving trouble but temporary repair effected.Rough check on provisions shows we have enough for forty five days. We hope it will not take us as long as that.

1500   Sighted two large whales.

1700   Crew bathed; shark watch kept. Exercise very welcome after cramped positions in boat. This bathing was adopted as a daily practice when possible. Crew encouraged to swim once round the boat for exercise and also to scrape marine growth off the boat bottom.

Wed. 11 March

0130   Ran into heavy thunderstorm. A fireball rested on the boat for a few seconds only a couple of feet away from the crew. It took the form of a bright light and was presumably caused by a static charge. Lightening was flashing all round the boat incessantly and the noise was terrific. No damage, no casualties. Began to run before Northwest wind but rudder came adrift so hove to and spent another miserable night.

0830   Serious repairs began on rudder. The handle was cut off an eight inch screwdriver and the metal portion driven into the keel by Sgt Cosgrove and self. This was to serve as the bottom pintle. A quarter inch iron ringbolt was filed down to a spike and driven into the rudder for the centre attachment. Utilising the remains of the original fittings the rudder was then replaced, the operation being made very difficult by the heavy swell.   Tools used-3-cornered file, small screwdriver, cold chisel,small axe,Javanese knife and twine.   Sgts Corney and Lovegrove put up most magnificent effort in fixing rudder in face of great difficulties.Their language was in proportion to their success.

Thurs. 12 Mar.

0230   Ran into thunderstorm which gave us a sailing breeze. Course SE.Rudder came adrift again so carried on steering by oar but boat very difficult to hold, so limited spells to 15 minutes.

0600   Rudder repaired. A comparatively simple job this time.

0900   On our way to a slight breeze. Although the general course has been SE we have been close hauled most of the time. Can Mr Bartholomew be wrong?

Fri. 13 Mar.

0300   Got a good wind then lost rudder again. Only to be expected on a day like this. When we tried to repair the rudder we found that the metal pintle had dropped out ,so we had to make a wooden one.

1200   Estimated noon position 210 miles on track to Roebourne but longtitude very doubtful.   Becalmed since 1130, so lay sweating under the awning. A shark paid us a visit during the afternoon.Fired about 20 rounds of.303 at it but it was too deep.

1630   More trouble with the rudder.

Sat. 14 Mar.

0715   Extra ration of water from barrel into which a cake of Lifebuoy soap had fallen a few days previously. This was intended as a laxative as we had no number 9's on board and most of the crew were suffering from constipation. Results not all we hoped for.

1730   Seven days at sea and Saturday night ! Extra rations and a tot of whisky issued. drank the King's health and followed up with " Sweethearts and wives". Youngest member Sgt Snook called to reply to toast but for once words failed him. The crew has become more acclimatised to living in an open boat, but it is obvious from various conversations how few realise the hazards of this voyage.Some people seem to think that they are being taken for a nice pleasure trip and that there is no need for them to exert themselves.Luckily these are very few and morale is generally high.

Sun. 15 Mar.

0630   Rudder repaired.

1200   As the navigator gets more proficient so the results become less optimistic .Estimated noon position 111 degrees East 10 degrees South.

Mon 16.Mar.
Fair sailing all day in choppy sea with big swell running. Sky gives indication of coming storm.

Tue. 17 Mar.
Storm has not materialised but that has not prevented the rudder from parting company with the sternpost. The two chippies got it fixed again.

Wed. 18 Mar.

Have been befriended by a seabird, who sits on the rudder head performing amazing balancing feats. He is however inclined to peck away the binding around the tiller. Received a visit from a shark. This time the first lieutenant put a .38 bullet into him.Most of the crew suffering from pimples on the posterior. These very painful when at the tiller as we have no Rumbold upholstery on the quarter deck.Cures for pimples were " Mercurocrome", of which there was a small bottle on board, and sun bathing. Former cure produced some astonishing sights while the latter was apt to be painful if applied for too long a time.

Thurs. 19 Mar.

Very light sailing conditions with sea still choppy. Crews sleeping quarters rearranged to take some weight out of the bows.Positions were then two in the bows where they always got wet if there was any sea running; two on the thwart abaft the mast; two on the next thwart aft; two on the benches amidships and four in the stern. A small snack [two biscuits and two sardines or a little potted meat and a mouthful of water] being issued at noon each day. This gives us something to look forward to and helps pass the time.

Fri. 20 Mar.

0100   Becalmed with very heavy rainstorms all around. These eventually met overhead and a good water catchment was made. Under way soon after dawn. One of the "Queens" garters, type Barbara, hoisted on the signal halyard. Wind from the SSE as usual in this bloody ocean.

1630   Wind increasing and heavy clouds forming.

1800   Wind dropped and rain storms visible. Another foul night. Pouring rain and no wind. Whisky passed round to keep out the wet and cold and to enable us to sleep in spite of the discomfort.

Sat. 21 Mar.

0630   Under way, breeze freshening.

1830   Had to heave to as we were shipping water over the bows faster than we could bale. The boat started to become waterlogged and the lee gunwale remained awash. As soon as we hove to the rudder came adrift. Our position is pretty serious. The "Saturday night at Sea "customs were observed with the evening meal.

1030   Rudder fixed. This was a very difficult job owing to the mountainous seas and the very sharp movement of the boat. More praise to the   chippies. Under way again making about 5 - 7 knots. A very wet process.

1130   Hove to again as sea and wind too great. There is no reefing device on these sails and we cannot afford to run before the wind which is from the SW. Found that even with the sea anchor streamed, the "Scorpion " still insists on lying beam on to the sea and wind, so hoisted sail and put jib aback. This made her ride easier and she was actually   making headway without a rudder which, of course, had come adrift again. Our actual track was E by S, speed approx. one and a half knots. According to our sailing plan, we were about half way to Roebourne. Another foul night but everyone taking it very well. Still think in most cases it is a question of " where ignorance is bliss" Am later proved right.

Mon. 23 Mar.

0630   Wind dropped sufficiently to start sailing again as soon as rudder was fixed. Found we had to jettison three water barrels as sea water had got into them.

1200   Rudder came adrift again. Position 113 degrees East, 14 degrees 15 mins South. Very strong repairs made to rudder.

1445   Under way. Sun coming out which enables us to dry one or two garments. 1st Lieut. and I sharing all watches at the helm. Sea running very high. Everyone given two Quinine tablets as a precaution against the recent wettings.

Tues. 24 Mar.

0630   A gentle days sailing with a favourable wind. Sea going down but still coming on board every now and then.

Wed. 25 Mar.

1200   Becalmed. Most uncomfortable in the swell which is still very heavy. Will we never get a real break in the way of constant wind ? Mr. Bartholomew is a complete liar about winds in this part of the world. I bet he has never been here. Think there are grounds for an action against him as he is misleading schoolchildren.

Thur. 26 Mar.

Under way most of the day but only just. Luckily there is quite a lot of cloud about so it is not too hot. Had a really thorough check of the foodstuffs and found that we are very well placed,there being enough to enable us to increase rations and still

10

have plenty in hand. This is a great relief. Also a number of delicacies such as canned plums and tomatoes were found.

Fri. 27 Mar.

Still becalmed. Sea like glass. We have been adopted by another sea bird. Noon position showed that we have drifted North, but some doubts expressed as to the accuracy of the sight. Crew playing crosswords to pass the time.

Sat. 28 Mar.

Same old calm. Noon position shows a further drift to the North but everyone refuses to believe the Navigator who keeps his temper remarkably well. General impression is that sextant suffered damage during the gale.

Sun. 29 Mar.

Becalmed. Rations reduced to former scale as things do not look too good. A few more of these calms and we would be up the creek. Northerly drift still apparent but everyone except navigator expressing silent disbelief. Navigator's attitude is "take it or leave it." 1st Lieut. nice and gloomy about chances of reaching Australia. As the diarist said ' Mr Streatfeild's morale very low."Had to give him [Stretty] a pep talk. Not the first, but rather excelled myself this time.

Mon.30 Mar.
"As idle as a painted ship..." Am not at all surprised that the Ancient Mariner went nuts. Noon position now confirms the northerly drift. This is very upsetting as, if this current has been present all the time, our sailing plot , which has been used as a check on our estimated position, is quite false. The navigator,with

11

great forebearance, has not yet remarked " I told you so." Northerly drift since 28 March reckoned at 82 miles.

Tues. 31 Mar.

Still becalmed. Further check of rations shows that the tinned fruit and some of the rations are going bad through heat, rust and being shaken about. In view of our drift, the uncertainty of our position and lack of progress generally, things are starting to look most unpleasant. A blissful air of unconcern reigns forward. During this calm we have rigged the awning after breakfast and organised games competitions between the quarter deck and fo'castle. These have kept us occupied and helped to pass the time; but we found that the mental exercise made us very hungry and the talking and arguing brought on a thirst. These are easier to bear than monotony.

Wed. 1 Apr.

Still becalmed and not many April Fool jokes. The penalty for April Fools, about ships or land, was loss of beer ration for rest of the voyage. Slight breeze sprang up during the morning. No notice taken in spite of MacDonald's continuous comments as we were busy with the finals of the "Letters Competition" Eventually,MacDonald became so insistent that we had to set sail. Score in competition eight all and one to play. Wind increased from NW during the afternoon. Is this our break?

Thur. 2 Apr.

Still sailing at dawn. Noon position puts us about 390 miles from Roebourne. Wind has backed and we are close hauled again.Obviously Mr. Bartholomew is a liar of the first water and has no idea what he is talking about. We still have our bird companions.

Fri. 3 Apr.

Wind fresh but variable. Course SSW. Sgt Haynes, i/c house,declared closing time at sunset as he has rigged his bed there.

Sat. 4 Apr.

Sailing comfortably but course still W of S. The " Scorpion" will not sail at all close to the wind, so we are making our Southing while we can. We have been joined by another bird. If this goes on we will become an aviary. They are the most peculiar creatures. Apparently they do not keep regular meal times and they are very tame. Also they keep their balance remarkably well for web footed birds, even when asleep, but if a particularly sharp roll almost upsets one of them, it always puts the blame on its companion. Perhaps everything goes nuts in the Indian Ocean.Had an issue of soi-desant Creme de Menthe for the "Saturday Night " celebration. A most peculiar concoction, later identified as a patent cough cure.

Sun. 5 Apr.

Nothing of interest. Wind freshening.

Mon. 6 Apr.

1200   Wind veered enough for us to make due East. We do not want to go Westwards more than we can help. Wind dropped in the afternoon.

Tue. 7 Apr.

0345   Put about to SSW as wind backed. Had to pinch to make that course but better than making NE.

2300   Becalmed.

Wed. 8 Apr.

1200   Becalmed all morning but noon position shows us 140 miles from Barrow Island and 180 from Onslow. Smoked last cigarette this evening. Had made contract with four members of the crew to save their butts. These were carefully saved and kept in a tin. It meant that I could have an occasional pipe. Will never again despise old men picking up fag ends from the gutter. I know just how they feel.

Thur. 9 Apr.

Becalmed. Young whale 50 to 60 feet long or about twice the size of the "Scorpion" surfaced about 200 yards away and decided to give us a close inspection. Eventually came to rest lying in a curve with its tail under the boat and poked its head out of the water certainly not more than three feet from the rudder. We could see the eye and mouth under water. "What does one do next?" We all hoped it would not become playful or try to make its toilet on the bottom of the boat and luckily, after looking at us for about half a minute which seemed like half an age, it submerged and went to join another whale which looks about four times as big. I hope the other one was its mother and that she "tore him off a strip" for going and staring at strangers.   When we had regained the power of movement we passed around a bottle of Australian 3 Star brandy which we had kept for an emergency, after which we did not care if we saw elephants pink or otherwise flying over us in

14

tight formation.Wind sprang up in the afternoon, probably as a result of this mornings vertical breeze, but possibly as a result of hoisting red garter in place of "Barbara".

Fri. 10 Apr.

Wind strong and increasing in force. Sea also getting up.Unfortunately wind is from SE so we have to tack and pinch to make E and W of S. As the "Scorpion" will not go about in a seaway, we have to wear ship every time and it is tantalising to see the speed she gets up with the wind abaft the beam. 1st Lieut. and self sharing watches on the tiller. We demand extra issue of food to keep us awake and were allowed to open a tin of ships biscuits.Found these very palatable and also a magnificent laxative,presumably due to increased bulk. Rest of the crew dodging waves or trying to.

Sat. 11 Apr.

Wind, which reached gale force during the night now moderating but considerable sea running. Lack of swell and shortness of sea make me think that we are East of North West Cape.

1200   Noon position shows plenty of Easting but only 13 miles of Southing. This not compatible with sailing plot. Reviled navigator, who both kept his temper and refused to be shaken from his calculations. He was right of course. Got inspected by another whale during the afternoon, but from a safe distance , thank God. These visitations occur when I am trying to write up the Squadron history, so I am giving this up for the time being.

Sun. 12 Apr.

0600 Wind dropped until we barely made steerage way. Most of crew very depressed wondering whether we are going to have another long calm after the last gale.

1800 Becalmed.
Mon. 13 Apr.

During daylight catspaw kept us moving, it is better to pretend to sail than lie about doing nothing. Boat making water fast. The last gale must have opened up a seam.Becalmed after sunset.

Tue. 14 Apr.

1200 Noon position 115 degrees 45 mins. E, 20 degrees 9 mins. S. We are now on the same latitude as Port Headland. Wind sprang up during the afternoon. Squadron colour garters hoisted in place of red one.

Wed. 15 Apr.

1200 Noon position shows that we have made 45 miles Easting. Regard this as extremely doubtful but am now wary of arguing with the navigator. Made some Easting during the day but breeze slight.

Thurs. 16 Apr.

Sgt. Corney swore he smelt spinifex on the dawn breeze. Soon he had everyone smelling something but, personally,put it down to the purser who suffers from flatulence. However, everyone very cheerful. Plans for the first meal ashore widely discussed.

1200   Noon position 118 degrees 50 min. East, 20 Degrees 11 min South or 30 miles from Port Headland, great excitement all round.

Fri. 17 Apr.

Dropped a bombshell this morning. Had spent a sleepless night working out times of sunrise and sunset during the past few days and had come to the conclusion that the recent large amount of Easting shown by the noon sight was due to my watch - the only one to survive, losing more than four minutes a day and that it may have lost as much as 40 minutes. This would put us 600 miles W of Port Headland, and about 250 miles W of the Western-most point of Australia. Rations, water and beer cut down, and an accurate check shows that we can last for another six weeks on the new scale. We shall all be in pretty poor condition by the end of that time. Thank God the water will last that time as it is one of the most important items, ranking equally with the beer. A breeze sprang up the morning and lasted until evening. We were becalmed by sunset and tried to row, but we were already so weak from six weeks on the boat that it was not very effective.

Sat. 18 Apr.

0200   Breeze sprang up. Much seaweed noticed but nobody dares say whether it indicates the proximity of land or whether it is commonly found right out to sea. We assume the latter to avoid disappointment. A swallow tail butterfly seen during the afternoon. That must mean that we are somewhere near land.

Sun. 19 Apr.

0300   Wind sprang up. If we do 10 miles a day in the right direction our rations will last out, even if we are right out to sea.

17

During the day several butterflies seen and some new type of jellyfish. Even I think we must be nearer land than I feared, but still dare not increase rations.

2230   Most members of the boat thought they heard a motor working, possibly a small motor boat. Lit a distress flare but had no reply.

Mon. 20 Apr.

0200   1st Lieutenant electrified everyone by shouting "Land ho".Sure enough there was a beach about 50 yards away.It appeared to be a small island and as the only island marked on our map was Barrow Island, which was quite a large piece of land, we reckoned that this was part of the mainland and decided to carry on until we could make certain. We soon discovered that we were surrounded by small islands and reefs which we had crossed at high water and which were now appearing as the tide went down, so we decided to wait for the dawn. Daylight showed us a sea dotted with small islands but no mainland; so we   put ashore at the point where we had first struck land, almost too literally, which we found to be Frazer Islet from a plate on a beacon which had been erected there. This did not convey much to anyone but, the mere fact that it was land, was very heartening.

0730   Put foot on dry land for first time since 7 March, our 45th day at sea. All members of the crew very weak but looking forward to a hot breakfast. Food issued ad lib and cocoa made, but people found that they could not eat as much as they thought, with the exception of the 1st Lieutenant who proved a fine trencherman. Purser feeling sick, probably reaction but may be the sight of so much food being issued at one meal.

1000   Navigator reported finding a chart [general navigation] of the world in the boat. We would- after 45 days. Chart showed we had reached Dampier Archipeligo between Onslow and Roebourne, so we decided to make for the mainland not too far distant.

1030   Set sail, course SSE.

1300   Sighted mainland or perhaps Barrow Island. Hard to tell, but think it is the mainland. Later proved correct.

1500   Altered course NE along coast. Winds appear favourable for us to   reach Roebourne. Sighted unidentified aircraft high about 10 miles to the West. Probably a Catalina. Flashed mirror and waved clothing but failed to attract attention. Some people rather disappointed, but general feeling that we have reached Australia by the grace of God and little else matters. Also if Catalinas are flying about, the Japs are not in occupation of the coast.

1600   Anchored in the lee of a small island as not considered safe to carry on through the reefs at night. Spent the night ashore after a hot meal. What a joy to lie on a stationary bed and a soft one too. Sgt. Corney made up Spinifex mattresses. His sense of smell was proved to be in good working order and accusations against purser withdrawn.

Tue. 21 Apr.

Boat grounded on ebb tide so crew spent morning ashore fishing from beach.Several Butterfish caught and cooked for an early lunch. Called island "Butterfish Island" as a result. Fish dammed good to eat after tinned food. Found boat leaking all along one of the starboard strakes.

19

1145   Underway, course NE.

1230   Sighted several kangaroos ashore. This proves that we are off the mainland and also indicates the presence of fresh water in the neighbourhood. A suspected water tank and pump turned out to be a tree.

1430   Flying boat [Catalina of Patrol Squadron 101, US Navy] appeared dead ahead at about 1500 feet. Pyjama jacket hoisted to peak in best "Razzle" style and all members of crew waved clothing etc. Afterwards learnt that Catalina crew thought we were having a free fight. After much signalling persuaded Catalina to alight but its crew very suspicious and displayed artillery. After exchange of semaphore signals [of a sort]I swam over to the flying boat, beating all existing records for ocean swimming in my anxiety to dodge any sharks that might be around. Was given a rope to hang on to but, in spite of the fact that I was mother naked, except for my beard, I was menaced by a man with a Colt .45 who would not let me on board until he was satisfied that I was harmless. Maybe he was right, but someone ought to have told him about sharks. Was told our position was about 50 miles from Roebourne. Captain of aircraft offered to take six of us off to their base, but only three of crew accepted the offer, Sgts. Cosgrove, Longmore and Haynes. Remainder determined to sail the "Scorpion" into port.
1700   Anchored for the night in a creek. Intended having a bit of a party since we had so much liquor left, but, after an enormous meal, everyone felt drowsy and went to sleep.

Wed. 22 Apr.

0830   Set off again. Decided to call our stopping place "Catalina Creek" but some members of the crew gave it a less euphonious name owing to the increased bowel activity caused by large meals.Continued on NE course and expected to turn East fairly soon; but as each headland was passed another was raised. However; no alarm was felt as food and drink was plentiful and we were off the mainland.

1200   Noon position gave our latitude just North of the Fortescue River, much further from Roebourne than we thought. If latitude 5 miles out, we should be much nearer Roebourne, in fact where we estimate we should be.   For a change we take the optimistic view.

1230   Catalina appeared from SW and made towards us. This time we displayed little interest, thinking that the Catalina was merely being curious.   The Catalina however, alighted and signalled that she had orders to take off all remaining crew. Great disappointment as, having got so far, it seemed a pity not to complete the trip. Lowered sail, unstepped the mast and gathered all belongings, such as they were.

1300   Crew transferred to flying boat and "Scorpion " set adrift.Unfortunately, in the hurry, Squadron shield [Scorpion embossed in copper on a wooden plinth] was left in the forward locker. Had intended hoisting this to masthead as we sailed into port.Discovered that information given on previous day regarding our position was inaccurate and that we were nearly 100 miles from Roebourne. So after 47 days, having sailed approximately 1500 statute miles, leaking like a sieve but still serviceable, with a jury rudder fitting in use since the second day, our HMRAFS "Scorpion" was cast adrift off the NW coast of Australia without the honour of being sailed into port. She was a cow into wind and would not go about without assistance, but she was very strong and a magnificent sea boat. No member of the crew wishes to make another trip like that, but, if fate should ever decree that if any of us are again at sea in an open boat, we all pray that it will will be as good as " Scorpion"

EPILOGUE.

The crew of the "Scorpion" spent the night on 22/23 April on board USS "Childs", the captain Lieut Commander Frank O'Beirne USN, who was the pilot of the Catalina which picked up the main party on 22 April. Great hospitality was shown and everyone was made very comfortable.

On April 23 the whole party was flown down to Perth in another Catalina. OC 84 Squadron got in touch with the US Naval authorities through the Air Officer Commanding the Western Area, Air Commodore de la Rue, RAAF and arrangements were made for a US submarine, the "Sturgeon" to call at "Scorpion Cove" Java on her way back from Corregidor and attempt to pick up the 84 Squadron aircrews who had been left there with orders to wait for two months if possible.

The "Sturgeon " went into the cove on the night of Thursday 30 April and sent her boat within 50 yards of the beach. The officer in charge of the boat, who had been notified of the signal arrangements, flashed the recognition signal and later hailed, but got no reply. A hand searchlight was then shone ashore, but all that was seen was a deserted lean-to. There was no sign of any cross of stones on the beach, denoting a voluntary departure, so the fate of the stranded aircrews of the squadron is problematical. Thus, apart from personal satisfaction and the escape of twelve members of the squadron, the voyage of the "Scorpion" was a failure; for, although help was sent within the time limit, rescue was not effected.

The Queens Garters.

Sqn Ldr Passmore, Fg Offr Streatfeild and Plt Offr Turner called their [Blenheim] aircraft "Queen of Shaibah ". "Stretty" carried a selection of feminine garters around with him which were put on the Pitout head fairing when going on an operational flight or on a special occasion. During the voyage the garters were used as pennants and as one set failed to produce a favourable wind another set would be hoisted. The garters had nothing to do with Streatfeild's morals.

Our Feathered Friends.

These were a type of deep sea gull. Owing to lack of human contact they were very tame and even if knocked off their perch for becoming too free with their beaks or for insanitary habits, they would come back for more. Their first efforts at deck landings were pretty poor; but they improved with practice until they were able to make landings with negative ground speed.

Other birds seen were Stormy Peterels, Man o' War birds,Albatross, some curious gulls with a long tail feather and some small sea birds which looked like sand martins.

Flying Fish.

From a close and prolonged study it appears that these fish always leave the water into the wind. The 'wings' are used to keep the body of the fish airborne; but, as the tail touches the water, it gives a few flicks thus regaining flying speed and lifting the whole fish clear of the water again. This flicking of the tail causes the whole fish to shimmer and gives the appearance of flying. On one or two occasions the 'flying fish' turned out to be young squid. These would leap out of the water to a height of 6 to 8 feet and, on one occasion, one came aboard, striking the 1st Lieut. a shrewd blow on the ear.

Other denizens of the deep seen during the voyage were sharks with their pilot fish, whales(and how) , porpoises, dugongs (sea cow), tunny, sting rays, skipjacks, blue mackerel, garfish, snappers, sea snakes, butterfish, turtles and a variety of jellyfish including blue -bottles.

In order to get the most out of every meal it became a habit to lick one's plate clean. This became a bit awkward when our beards grew, but the habit persisted and we had to watch ourselves very closely when we got back to civilisation. Also there was great competition to get any tins after their contents had been dished out in the hopes of finding a few scraps in the less accessible corners. Sgt Cosgrove earned himself the nickname of the " Alley Cat " from his habit of begging twice scoured tins and opening them out flat with a tin opener to get at any bits which could not be extracted with a knife, he was lucky not to get lead poisoning.

J.R.Jeudwine W/Cdr.   1942

NOTES AND COMMENTS ON THE LOG OF THE 'SCORPION'

1.   After the war the Japanese submarine seen on 9 March was identified as being under the command of Captain Katsuo Ohashi. He was killed before the end of the war. His brother Mr. Yasutoshi Ohashi was contacted and was presented with a book as a token of friendship. The presentation was made in Canberra, Australia, on 31 March 1987 by Air Vice-Marshal Bill Collings and was attended by Athel Snook [Ref. Canberra Times March 31 1987] According to his brother Captain Ohashi had deliberated for some time as to what to do about the lifeboat and its crew. Taking prisoners was out of the question, and in spite of the urging of some of his crew, refused to machine gun the boat.

2.   On 14 and 22 March the log has entries indicating that some of the crew did not seem to understand how serious their position was. This was refuted by John Lovegrove in a document he prepared after reaching Australia. He writes..." I feel, at this stage, the CO had under-estimated the Australian capacity of outwardly treating adversity lightly but inwardly seriously. " In this document he also refuted the statement that only the CO and Streatfeild had

had any sailing experience, stating that both he and Snook had sailed small boats extensively in Perth before the war and that they contributed to sailing knowledge during the voyage.

3. Lovegrove offers the theory that their landfall at Fraser Islet was in fact Mary Anne Island in the Mary Anne Passage, even though the island bore a beacon with the name Fraser Islet. Efforts by Lovegrove and Peter Haynes to locate this island, over a ten year period, proved unsuccessful. The maritime authorities have denied all knowledge of a "Fraser Islet". In an interview with Peter Haynes in February 1997, he described the beacon and confirmed the presence of the nameplate. The position of Mary Anne Island roughly agrees with the position given by the Catalina pilot who picked them up, thus the existence of Fraser Islet remains a mystery.

4. In his summary of the voyage Lovegrove wrote as follows:

" I consider that every member of the crew contributed in their own way to the success of the trip. I give full marks to the Skipper W/Cdr Jeudwine and 2nd in Command S/Ldr. Passmore for the way they maintained discipline without undue regimentation. There were times when conditions became almost intolerable but I never heard any real dissension amongst the crew. Perhaps the only time there were any arguments was during our word games competitions between Port and Starboard watches and this was in fun but the competition was very intense. For what it is worth 'The proof of the pudding is in the eating', we all remained good friends after being thrown together in limited space under frightful conditions for 47 days."

5. Peter Haynes confirmed Lovegrove's comments, adding that though the CO remained fairly aloof he joined in the " Saturday Night at Sea " celebrations and competitions with gusto.

6. The Catalina flyingboat which picked up the crew was flown by 20 year old Paul Stevens, USN, who later apologised for his lack of hospitality when Jeudwine attempted to board the Catalina. He wrote " at that time caution seemed the best policy. The

25

Japanese had run wild since December 1941 and they used many dirty tricks to obtain their goals. Actually, flying a PBY Catalina in those days one looked over one's shoulder constantly." Paul Stevens retired as a Captain, US Navy and settled in Nashville, Tennesee.

7. During the period March 24 to 26 the "Scorpion" was becalmed or sailing in gentle breezes but in very heavy swell. At this time the Australian coast at Port Headland was being battered by a cyclone with winds to 120 miles per hour with a Barometric pressure of 938 and sea level two metres above predicted high water level. Rainfall was 299mm or nearly 12 inches. Had "Scorpion" progressed further on her voyage she would never have survived the cyclone.

8. The party left behind at "Scorpion Cove" was under the charge of P/O Keble-White, and numbered about 40 NCO's, P/O's Milsom and Miller and four transport drivers. Keble-White wrote later - "The party numbered about 50, and though they had been harrassed by the enemy from the time they set foot in Malaya spirits ran surprisingly high. We had no aeroplanes, they were lost, what were left of them, at Kalajati a week earlier, we had no ships, the last had left several days previously, and owing to the enemy having gained mastery of the sea and sky, no more were expected; but we had the ships lifeboat from a sunken KPM ship, and we had a good hiding place on the beach where we could wait for relief which he (Jeudwine) promised to send. That the only link with our friends could fail was a thought which did not enter our heads, that entirely false optimism which seems to pervade Englishmen facing the most unfavourable odd, was running high and bets were being laid as to the time we should have to wait. Jeudwine thought he could reach Australia in three weeks, but gave me instructions to remain where we were for two months; signals were arranged to be used between the relieving party and ourselves, and, on the evening of March 7th our only hope set sail, twelve men in a motor-less keel-less boat, with a very small sail of unique design." He

continues... "Although the quantity [of stores] looked large while in cases, it is surprising how much is required for forty odd men for two months. Working on this basis we found we could only run to two meals per day about three and a half ounces of bully beef per man per day, plus four issue biscuits, tea twice a day and an occasional addition of a tin of tomatoes. Besides the food we had a large stock of American canned beer, about 1100 cans in all, and this was issued daily while it lasted. Our medical supplies were totally inadequate, and comprised a small Red Cross First Aid bag, we had no laxatives, no quinine and only a limited quantity of antiseptic."

Keble-White continues..." After considering the rather critical position with the other officers, I decided that I must attempt to augment our stores with some form of bulk food. Eight NCO's volunteered to return to the mainland and P/O Milsom took a party up to the lighthouse to get bananas. Both parties were abortive, owing to the presence of Japanese forces, and in the case of the NCO's, four failed to return having been captured. Two months later we were very distressed to hear that the missing four had been executed. As a result of this unpleasant episode we had to confine ourselves to the beach, and furthermore, great care had to be taken with regard to noise and smoke from fires. Any building work was seriously curtailed and our foraging field was reduced to the sea only............ As the days dragged by and our plight grew worse, our spirits sank, and when, on 20th April we were discovered by a half-caste Dutch official, we were glad to give ourselves up. We only had four days rations left and some of the lads were, by this time, very ill."

What followed for this unfortunate party were threats of execution, beatings, forced labour, starvation and three years of severe deprivation.

The "Scorpion " reached Australia two days after the ground party was taken into captivity.

END

27

Appendix Two

Summary of operations carried out by Wg Cdr Jeudwine
with Bomber Command during the period 3.12.43 to 17.9.44

Date	Aircraft		Target	Duration	Remarks
03/12/43	Lanc	DV326	Leipzig	7h30m	2nd pilot
20/12/43	"N"	LM419	Frankfurt	5h55	
29/12/43		LM419	Berlin	7h05	
02/01/44		LM419	Berlin	7h30	
28/01/44	"A"	LL778	Berlin	7h35	
15/02/44		LL778	Berlin	7h10	
20/02/44		LL778	Stuttgart	7h00	
24/02/44		LL778	Schweinfurt	8h15	
01/03/44		LL778	Stuttgart	8h25	
10/03/44		LL778	Chateauroux	5h50	Controller
24/03/44		LL778	Berlin	7h10	
05/04/44		LL778	Toulouse	7h45	Controller
10/04/44		LL778	Tours	6h10	Controller
26/04/44		LL778	Schweinfurt	9h00	
01/05/44		LL778	Toulouse	8h00	
07/05/44		LL778	Salbris	5h45	Controller
11/05/44		LL778	Bg Leopold	2h05	Early return
19/05/44	"A"	ND840	Tours	5h45	Controller
22/05/44		ND840	Brunswick	5h45	Controller
27/05/44		ND840	Morsaline gun	3h45	Controller
01/06/44	"Y"	NE167	Saumur	6h00	Controller
05/06/44		NE167	La Pernelle	4h10	Controller
08/06/44	Mos	DZ521	Pontaubault	3h45	Controller
09/06/44		DZ521	Etampes	3h05	Controller
12/06/44		DZ521	Caen	?	Controller
14/06/44	Mos	DZ415	Aunay/Odon	3h35	Marker
21/06/44		?	Scholven	?	Controller
24/06/44		?	Prouville	?	Controller
14/07/44	P38	Lightning	Villeneuve	?	Late on target
18/07/44	P38	Lightning	Revigny	?	Controller
17/09/44		Lanc ?	Boulogne	?	Observer

1 a

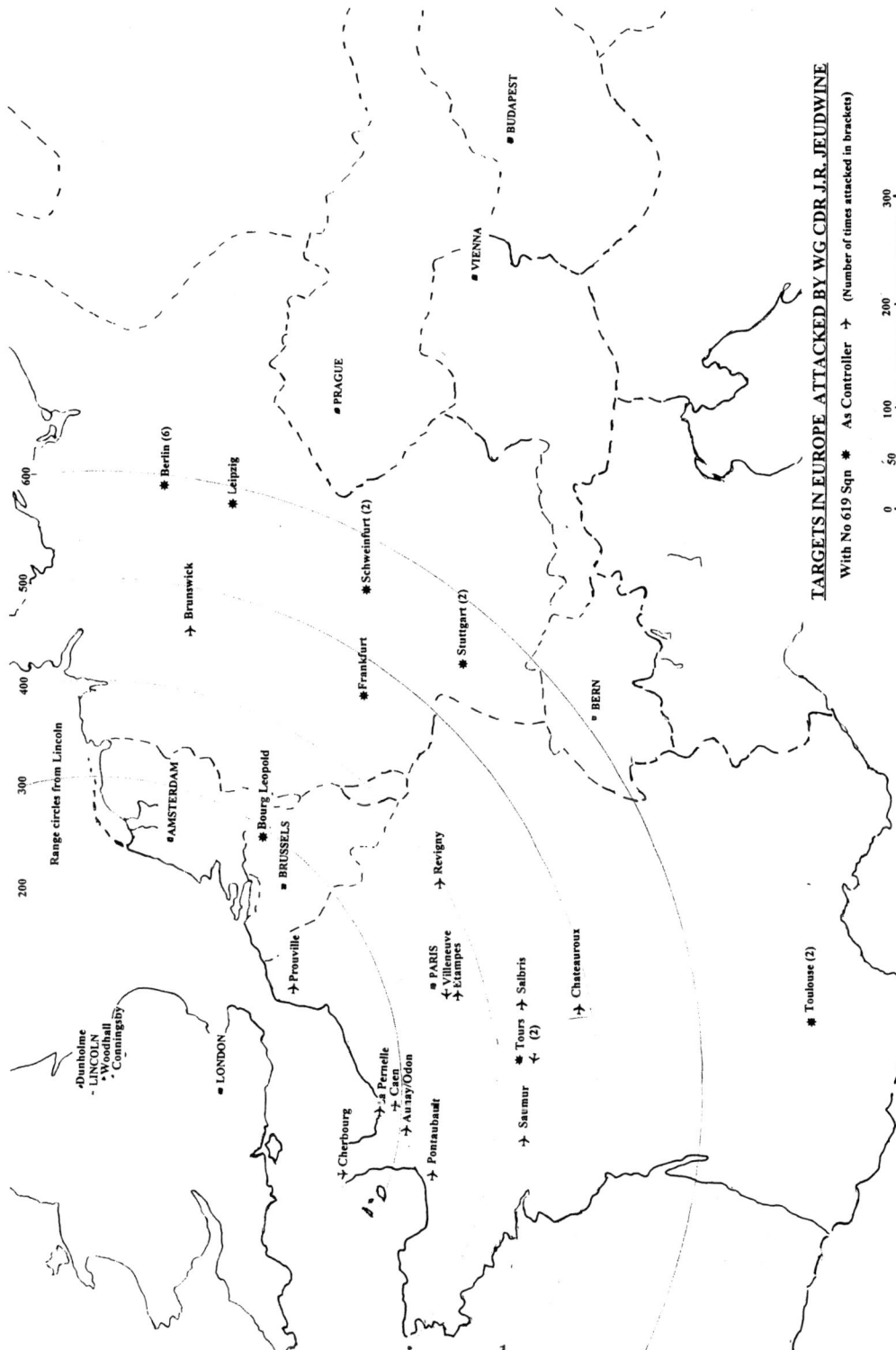

TARGETS IN EUROPE ATTACKED BY WG CDR J.R. JEUDWINE

With No 619 Sqn ✱   As Controller ✈   (Number of times attacked in brackets)

Range circles from Lincoln

✱ BUDAPEST

✱ VIENNA

✱ PRAGUE

✱ Berlin (6)

✱ Leipzig

✈ Brunswick

✱ Schweinfurt (2)

✱ Stuttgart (2)

✱ Frankfurt

✱ BERN

✱ AMSTERDAM

✱ Bourg Leopold

▪ BRUSSELS

✈ Revigny

✈ Prouville

▪ PARIS
✈ Villeneuve
✈ Étampes

✈ Salbris

✈ Chateauroux

✱ Toulouse (2)

▪ LONDON

▪ Dunholme
- LINCOLN
 ▪ Woodhall
 ▪ Coningsby

✈ Cherbourg
✈ La Pernelle
✈ Caen
✈ Auuay/Odon

✈ Pontaubault

✈ Saumur ✱ Tours ✈ Salbris
 ✈ (2)

0 50 100 200 300

BIBLIOGRAPHY

The authors have consulted many books and official records held at the Public Record Office (PRO) London. The following is a selection of the most frequently used material.

Title	Author(s)	Publisher
Battle for Pelambang	Kelley	Hale 1958
Bloody Shambles	Cull&Shores	Grubb Street
Bomber Command War Diaries	Middlebrook & Everitt	Penguin
British Naval Aviation 1917-1990	Sturtivant	Arms & Armour 1990
Fly Navy	Johnson	David& Charles
Hurricanes over the jungle	Kelley	Kimber 1977
Point Blank& Beyond	Lacey-Johnson	Airlife 1991
RAF Squadrons	Jefford	Airlife
The Desert Air War	Bickers	Leo Cooper
The Desert War	Bramall&Gilbert	Sidgwick & Jackson
The Enemy is Listening	Clayton	Hutchinson
The Forgotten Air Force	Probert	Brassey's
Journal of the RAF College Cranwell Autumn 1934		Gale & Polden
The Lancaster File	Halley	Air Britain 1985
The Scorpion's Sting	Neate	Air Britain 1994
There Shall Be Wings	Arthur	Coronet
The Army List 1915-1918		
The Medical Dictionary 1933/34		
The Navy List 1935-1939		

I

PRO Files
   Files consulted at the PRO were mainly in classes Air 14,
Air 24, Air 25, Air 27, Air 28, Air 29, and Air 40.
Squadron and Unit Operations Record Books (540s) examined
included:-

Air 14/868	5 Group Marking
Air 25/122	HQ 5 Group
Air 27/164	12 Sqn
27/696/7	84 Sqn
27/517	55 Sqn
27/2131	619 Sqn
27/2387	823 Sqn
27/688	83 Sqn
Air 28/706	Shandur
28/724	Strubby
28/228	Dunholme
28/955	Woodhall
28/171/2	Coningsby
28/493	Little Staughton
Air 29/457	ME Ferry Control Units
29/152	AM/WT Station Cairo
29/854	54 Base
29/3645	DD Sigs "Y"
29/685	70 OTU Kenya
Air 40/--	Intelligence Reports

L.L-J 1999

II